D0676782

Biblical Criticism and Heresy

in Milton

Biblical Criticism and Heresy

in Milton

GEORGE NEWTON CONKLIN

King's Crown Press

Columbia University, New York

1949

Copyright 1949 by

GEORGE NEWTON CONKLIN

.   KING'S CROWN PRESS

is a subsidiary imprint of Columbia University Press established for the purpose of making certain scholarly material
available at minimum cost.   Toward that end, the publishers
have adopted every reasonable economy except such as would
interfere with a legible format.   The work is presented sub-
stantially as submitted by the author, without the usual editorial and typographical attention of Columbia University
Press.

PUBLISHED IN GREAT BRITAIN AND INDIA
BY GEOFFREY CUMBERLEGE, OXFORD UNIVERSITY PRESS
LONDON AND BOMBAY

MANUFACTURED IN THE UNITED STATES OF AMERICA

To my father and mother
with gratitude

253890

Preface

THE PURPOSE of this study of some of the philological aspects of Milton's exegesis in his *De Doctrina Christiana* is to present the view that there is a likelihood that Milton's doctrinal heterodoxies may have derived largely from his method of Biblical criticism rather than from patristic, Renaissance, or rabbinical sources.

The strongest evidence for this contention is Milton's own insistence on the point. By an examination of the actual exegetical process of Milton's formulation of two unorthodox doctrines, I have attempted to verify Milton's avowal of complete and necessary independence in his theology as against indebtedness to the various sources suggested by contemporary critics.

Naturally, with so vast a body of theological material available to Milton, the question of his reading can scarcely be ignored. It is quite possible to assume that Milton, despite his claim of absolute originality, may merely have adapted his exegesis to support conclusions already derived from other sources. Indeed, such an assumption, in light of Milton's statement, must obviously be made before attributing his beliefs to any specific writer or writings.

The guiding hypothesis of the views expressed here, however, is that Milton's description of his method and purpose in the *De Doctrina* is the truth rather than subterfuge. Internal evidence in the actual treatise as well as the bibliocentric ideology and philological production of his age appear amply to support Milton's argument.

Doctrines of other writers, mainly Socinian, noticed here, therefore, have been cited as instances of derivation from comparable textual criticism rather than probable sources for Milton, even though the possibility of such extra-Biblical sources cannot be denied. Indeed, it is likely that Milton was familiar with Socinian exegesis; but there is in my opinion insufficient evidence to suggest that he was influenced by their doctrines.

Strictly speaking, the possibility of Milton's *subconscious* borrowings from other sources, suggested by at least one critic, cannot, I suppose, be eliminated. This, however, is a clinical rather than a critical question and may properly be left to the probings of psychologists.

Exact and final proof of the origin of Milton's departures from orthodoxy may never be established; but Milton's statement of originality in the matter should be at least regarded as significant, particularly since originality in Christian doctrine as revealed by Scripture was integral with his theology; and, in fact, for Milton, depended upon the Holy Spirit itself.

For the convenience of the reader who is not immediately familiar with the historical development of Biblical criticism and for whom such a frame of reference may be useful, a résumé of the main features of Renaissance Biblical scholarship has been included in the First Chapter. Although it is evident that this material is germane to Milton's critical equipment, it must be understood that it has been inserted with no idea of giving a proper history of the subject but merely to present some of the more significant historical features of the background of the

Biblical criticism familiar to Milton. To attempt more would be impertinent, not to say improper.

One other qualification seems necessary. Because of the stature of Harris Fletcher as a Milton critic and the consequent importance of his theory of the rabbinical influence on Milton, it has been necessary to examine his arguments in some detail. From this investigation it seems to be clear that Mr. Fletcher's thesis is neither proved nor plausible; but I would not wish to imply that his theory—any more than any other—is impossible. Possibilities and proofs are clearly different things.

This study was begun in 1938 under the late Frank Allen Patterson, of Columbia University. For the friendly encouragement I received while preparing it, I must especially thank Dr. Louis Finklestein, of the Jewish Theological Seminary; Dr. W. W. Rockwell, of Union Theological Seminary; and Professor O. J. Campbell, of Columbia University. For helping me to prepare my manuscript for the press, I am indebted to Professor D. L. Clark, of Columbia University, and particularly, to my friend and colleague, Professor T. J. Henney, of Wesleyan University.

I must also gratefully acknowledge the generous cooperation that I received at all times from the library staffs of Columbia University, Union Theological Seminary, the Jewish Theological Seminary of New York, General Theological Seminary, Yale University, New York Public Library, the British Museum, and Wesleyan University.

I am thoroughly indebted to Wesleyan University for a research grant and to Columbia University for a fellowship which have been indispensable to the accomplishment of this work. The English Department of the Graduate School and, in particular, Professors M. H. Nicolson and W. Haller have been a tower of strength to me. Their friendly aid in readmitting me into the academic world after four years of navy life has, in a very real sense, made it possible for me to finish this work.

It is to my wife, Elizabeth Lloyd Conklin, however, that I owe whatever may have been accomplished. Through her alone have I been able to return to the best of professions.

To be unaware of the limitations of a study of this sort is impossible, but it is nevertheless hoped that some of the suggestions advanced may prove useful to the company of Miltonists. For them, this study: *ego jam doctae pars quamlibet catervae*.

G. N. C.

Wesleyan University
Middletown, Connecticut
1948

Acknowledgments

Acknowledgment is here made of the courtesy of publishers and copyright owners in permitting me to quote from the following books: Harris Fletcher's *Milton's Rabbinical Readings*, The University of Illinois Press; David Masson's Life of John Milton, The Macmillan Company.

Contents

. . . . the study of scripture, (which
is the only true theology . . . .
                    "Hirelings."

I

Sacred Philology

TOWARD THE CLOSE of the Renaissance, not long after
the revolt of Copernicus, there began in Europe another
revolution equally profound and perhaps as consequential
in the history of Western thought. This second revolution, the origins of which may in fact be traced to the
medieval period, while less immediately spectacular than
the new view of the heavens, was nothing less than a re-
evaluation of the scriptural revelation of Christian theology, which brought about in turn a new view of God.
Not less significant than the change from geocentric to
heliocentric cosmos was the transition from a single doctrinal system based upon the unchallenged scriptural
text of St. Jerome to the various creeds to be derived from
sacred philology and new translations of the Bible.

The change from the medieval interpretative gloss *on*
a passage of Scripture to the new grammatical analysis
of the passage brought forth an entirely new question in
theology. The rhetorical commentaries of the earlier
period, generally concerned with delineating the intention
of a phrase and never questioning any matter of textual
integrity, gave way to the *disquisitiones philologicae* in
which all instances of textual corruption were investigated,
and the whole emphasis placed upon exact rendition. The
older query, so to speak, of "What does God mean here?"
became the far more arresting question, "What has God
said here?" Allegory, mystic paraphrase, tropology, and

the whole formal literature of interpretation were uncompromisingly attacked as doctrinal irrelevancies by syntax and lexicography. Grammar, not speculation, became the greatest heresy of the Christian world, and unhappily no fires could be kindled to consume the *rudimenta linguae* of Hebrew and Greek. The old rhetorical axiom, *est accentus velut anima vocis*, became a pivotal question of theology; for what was at stake now was not *vocis* but *Scripturarum*.

Now the seventeenth century, an era of enormous erudition almost wholly concerned with Biblical scholarship, following the twin *momenta* of Reformation and Humanism, stands in the history of Biblical study as the great age of sacred philology. When William Chillingworth announced his simple tenet of faith, "the Bible alone," there was immediately involved in the exposition of that bald conception not merely the familiar approach of the Puritans to the plain word of God, but rather, fed by the period's precocious outburst of linguistic learning, a formidable, complex, and brilliant quest for a final, proved, and irrefutable rendition of the Bible, the religion of Protestants.

Scholars and tinkers, doctors and divines, devoted their energies—their very lives—to this qualified exegesis, the new basis for doctrine. Orthodoxy found more proofs in better translation; Rome sought to re-establish her doctrinal authority by philological refutation of her opponents; while others formulated new articles of faith, new creeds, and new churches. Philology, suffering severe strains in syntax, served all; but when least fettered by traditional necessities, most drastically widened the essential dichotomy between objective grammatico-historical investigation and subjective Christian revelation.

Before the movement grew sterile and viciously pedantic, it brought forth some of the most creditable monuments of great scholarship and learning ever produced in Europe.[1]

This was the milieu in which John Milton produced his "methodical tractate" on Christian doctrine. Puritan in orientation, independent by instinct, Humanist and scholar by training, Milton, in his "diligent perusal" of Scripture, quite fully demonstrates the philological dilemma of his age. The heterodoxies that resulted from his theory and practice of Biblical criticism (liberal Puritan hermeneutics[2] plus philological exegesis) seem an inevitable corollary of that medium rather than a potpourri of directing influences from his catholic and constant reading. Numerous investigations of Milton's heresies have been made in recent years; and parallels, sources, and influences have been suggested in such volume that it has been possible to collate a considerable number of them as commonplaces of the times.[3]

But if Milton is to be believed in his solemn affirmation of originality and his repeated insistence that he followed no other sect or heresy[4] (and quite apart from his statement, his theory of criticism and exegetical methods strongly confirm his theologically necessary independence), the starting point for a consideration of Milton's deviations from accepted doctrine, despite the respectable collection of possible extra-Miltonic sources, should be most clearly evident in his specific derivations of belief from Scripture. For no matter what remarkable comparisons can be made with contemporary speculation (and unquestionably the Socinian output is particularly tempting in this respect),[5] Milton's positions depended first upon scriptural authority, and this under the guidance of no mortal.[6] Milton, it is true, for purposes of forensic embellishment frequently cited whatever contemporary authority was suitable for a specific contention; but these authorities merely supplement and never originate the scripturally founded truth in question.[7]

The importance of the *De Doctrina Christiana* as an illuminating and qualifying foundation for the theological conceptions inherent in *Paradise Lost* should surely be evident; and Kelley's work[8] is a long-needed, adequate, and (judging from recent criticism which attempts to ignore the plainly stated heresies of Milton)[9] necessary exposition of the point. What has not been sufficiently noticed, however, is Milton's expressed method of doctrinal derivation (pungently outlined in the Preface to the *De Doctrina* and consistently executed throughout the treatise) and the patent connection between his heresies and his "careful perusal and meditation of the Holy Scriptures themselves."[10] Because of its very purpose,[11] Milton's formulation of Christian doctrine cannot be analyzed in the same manner as his other prose tracts; it is not enough to characterize the *De Doctrina* as a mere private exercise largely modeled after Wollebius.[12] For whatever the structural outline and common orthodoxies (such as may be noted in Ames, Wollebius, Grotius, Gomarus, Ursinus, and others) of Milton's treatise, it contains, besides the more familiar antitrinitarian argument, two theses that, for sheer heterodoxy, go far beyond even the rampant *Fratres Poloni*.[13] These two beliefs are, in fact, so individual (one of them indeed appears to be uniquely Milton's) and so singular in textual genesis, namely, his mortalism[14] and his pantheistic materialism,[15] that parallels to the ideas in one case are rare and approximate,[16] and in the other simply nonexistent. It is to Milton's "rule of Scripture" and to his conception of interpretation that we must turn for explicit exposition of these extreme conclusions. With Milton's hermeneutics definitely propounded and his exegetical equipment and technique so manifest, there may be no great need to search for the sources of his theological irregularities. It is quite probable that the ideas, the reasoning, and the proofs are wholly Milton's; the parallels, wherever they occur, merely concidental. The authorship of the *Ars Logicae* and the partial draft of a Latin grammar, the cogent ability in Biblical Hebrew and Greek, the consecrated and conscientious seriousness of treatment, and what might be called Milton's hallmark, "the unwearied search after truth," are all thoroughly in evidence throughout the *De Doctrina*. By the very terms of his hermeneutics and the philological capability of his exegesis, Milton through his Biblical criticism developed alone, with Puritan independence and Renaissance talent, his system of Christian doctrine.

In examining Milton's Biblical criticism, attention must be given to the matter of Hebraica and the related question of his dependence on rabbinical commentaries. The distinguished labors of the Christian Hebraists[17] of the period, the lexicographic production of Buxtorf, Schindler, Leigh, and others, and the general familiarity of the age with rabbinical material warrant a careful appraisal of Harris Fletcher's hypothesis.[18] Although rabbis are not cited in the *De Doctrina*, there is an instance in one of the tracts[19] of Milton's looking to rabbinical exegesis for supporting evidence of his own conclusions.[20] The importance of the rabbis, so far as their pertinence to the subject of this study is concerned, lies solely in the question of their possible influence upon Milton's formulation of doctrine. The related question of their influence on *Paradise Lost* is another conjecture[21] and belongs, in fact, to a quite different type of criticism. Either the rabbis directly suggested aspects of theology to Milton or they did not; the latter alternative is the conviction here.

One of the intentions of this study is to suggest Milton's independence and ability as a Biblical scholar, and the direct bearing of his method of scriptural criticism upon the origin of his heterodoxies. By looking at his Biblical interpretation in light of the background of his age and particularly the philological scholarship available to him (while noting some points of its development), it is hoped that the examples of his exegetical practice discussed below may clarify the origin of his doctrines and show his theology to be independently adduced and beholden to none. Of his use of lexicons, grammatical notes, and exegetical aids of a linguistic nature, considerable probing will be done, not, however, to establish a source, but only to illuminate the production of the period and suggest Milton's probable method of working.

No attempt will be made to evaluate Milton's theology as such. This is manifestly the task of the theological historian. The scriptural origin and method of proof is the only approach to doctrine that is to be discussed. Again, because the ramifications of the whole conception of the Son and the doctrine of free will go beyond the strictly linguistic emphasis of this investigation, only the unorthodox doctrines of mortalism and materialism will be examined.

It is, of course, realized that the vastness of the exegetical material involved prohibits, short of a lifetime of study, anything more than a general familiarity with the field. Accordingly, it is only from Milton's immediate arguments and phrases that conclusions of any significance can possibly be deduced; necessarily this must be the emphasis, though on occasion wider speculation is sometimes made.

Although the study of sacred philology reached its zenith in the seventeenth century, Biblical textual criticism began in the era of the Reformation. (It should be remarked in passing that the single medieval effort toward an *apparatus criticus* for the Vulgate text, that of Nicholaus de Lyra's *Postilla in Universa Biblia*, achieved, through its use by Luther, no small notoriety in the sixteenth century and, in fact, played an influential part in the Reformation conception of accurate translation.)[22] The new Humanism, with its zealous emphasis on the acquisition of Greek[23] and manifest enthusiasm for philological learning of any sort, served as the catalyst for the textual study of Biblical Greek and Hebrew. In the rise of grammatico-historical exegesis, Renaissance and Reformation join forces.

The power of linguistic learning against Church polity had already been amply demonstrated by Valla,[24] while in Biblical studies the labors of such Humanists as Reuchlin and Erasmus paved the way for the philological study of Scripture by providing the first lexicographic tools[25] and textual canon for the subject.[26] Reuchlin,[27] because of his Hebrew studies and particularly because of his *De Rudimentis Hebraicis* (1506), merits his sobriquet of "the father of Hebrew learning" in the Christian Church; but it is to Erasmus that the greater achievement as principal founder of modern textual criticism must be assigned.[28] Erasmus's publication of the first edition of the Greek Testament in 1516[29] marks the commencement of a new era of theological study. In a very real sense, not only because of his forcible exposition of the errors of the schoolmen and repudiation of the exegetical infallibility of the Church, but also by his high competence in grammatical analysis of New Testament Greek,[30] Erasmus may be considered the first of the new critics who advanced the phalanx of grammar into the ranks of orthodox tradition.

The incalculable influence of Luther's Bible in effecting the triumph of Protestantism is widely recognized; but for the specific development being traced here, it is more important to note that it was largely through his enormous labors to make as true a translation as possible that a foundation was laid for the newer methods of criticism. Although possessing a limited knowledge of Hebrew and depending on the texts of the Vulgate, Septuagint, Erasmus's New Testament, and a few of the Latin Fathers, Luther received help from the mighty Melancthon,[31] and during the twelve years of composition, considerable aid from various rabbis. The principle of exact translation, the *point d'appui* of the later movement, no matter how praiseworthy the earlier work, was spread most effectively by Luther. Certainly, if only in terms of general circulation, the subsequent influence of Luther's studied translation of Scripture is second to none.

Far surpassing Luther in scholarship was his friend Melancthon.[32] A pupil of Reuchlin, and especially learned in Greek, Melancthon's thorough acquaintance with the original languages of Scripture made him a highly able exegete. His commentaries, though at times allegorical, usually followed the grammatico-historical method. Terry remarks that Melancthon clearly perceived the Hebraic character of New Testament Greek, and that his edition of the Septuagint (1545) was published with the idea of furthering this line of study.[33] It was Melancthon too who most succinctly epitomized the basic hypothesis of coming exegetes by his declaration, *"Ignavus in grammatica est ignavus in theologia."*[34] His words foreshadowed the theological failure as well as the critical success of the movement.

In the same period the Swiss reformers Zwingli, Oecalampodius, and others practiced a comparable criticism; but aside from advancing the general scriptural cause, they made no noteworthy linguistic progress. Conrad Pellicanus, of Zurich,[35] and Sebastian Münster,[36] however, have some claim to importance in the history of sacred philology, the former for his adherence to the literal sense and considerable use of rabbinic commentators for analysis of the Hebrew text and the latter for his authorship of numerous texts on Hebrew and Chaldee grammar. Pellicanus's translations of rabbinical commentary, if we can assume the accuracy of Imbonatus,[37] are fairly staggering in quantity.

Admittedly foremost of all the Reformation critics, though not the equal of Erasmus or Melancthon in matters of purely textual and philological analysis, was John Calvin. His style and method of exegesis, rather than singular syntactic discoveries, make his commentaries famous in the critical literature of Biblical study—not to say in the whole field of theology. Calvin is the great exponent of the plain and simple sense of Scripture theme (which we shall observe to a marked degree in Milton) in direct antithesis to the labored gloss of any sort. For Milton's theory of criticism, this aspect of Calvin's position is of chief importance. On the great inspiration of Calvin's criticism and his theological stature there is no need to digress. It is the actual practice of his exegesis, that bears at once on the development of later techniques of criticism, that is of moment for purposes of this emphasis.

Calvin's method was first to establish the plain sense and context of a passage. Little of other commentators and no mystical, allegorical, or forced exposition are interposed between commentary and Scripture. Brief and largely free from digression, the clarity of Calvin's exegesis did much to establish the notion of the essential simplicity of God's word and a corresponding suspicion of all elaborate glosses. Though perhaps closer to Grotius in actual method and to Chillingworth in conception, Milton's commentaries strongly resemble the tone of Calvin's in logical concision and assumption of textual clarity. Like Calvin and, unlike some of the later philologists, Milton in his examination of Scripture found nothing mystic in the text and followed consistently Calvin's dictum of interpretation which held that the first duty of an interpreter is to let his author say what he does say, instead of attributing to him what we think he ought to say.[38]

Besides Beza, Junius, and Tremellius, familiar as editors of the Bible most likely used by Milton,[39] there flourished in this period such distinguished expositors as Bucer, Flacius, Musculus, Peter Martyr, Cameron, Mercer, Camerarius, Brenz, Carlstadt, Marlorat, Agricola, and many others[40] who, in varying degree, advanced the movement of philological criticism. All agreed generally in the rejection of allegory and the fourfold sense; all were in revolt against Scholasticism, Church tradition, and patristic authority; and most, in practice, emphasized the literal sense. Significant too before the seventeenth century was the tremendous emphasis on translation of the Bible into modern languages, not to mention the polyglots of Antwerp and Nuremberg.[41]

The linguistic groundwork for the domination of sacred philology was completed by the end of the sixteenth century. The textual and grammatical accomplishments of the preparatory period were noteworthy but scarcely developed to the point of a separate science. Nevertheless, the sterility of medieval exegesis[42] had ended; the Lutherans had broken away from the tradition and authority of the Church; and the Reform theologians had begun the approach to Scripture in the spirit of free criticism. The dynamic age of Milton with its enormous production of revolutionary criticism and doctrine was on the way.

If the Renaissance stimulus to the linguistic aspects of Reformation exegesis leads one to characterize the beginnings of sacred philology as humanistic, then the productivity of the seventeenth century can only be described as a veritable *furor philologicus*. Whole sections of library stacks would be required to shelve even a decades's output, and the recorded exegetical bibliography of the whole age requires several volumes. It is usual in our times to regard this whole corpus of criticism as sterile scholia, mere theological nugae, or, at best, an unnecessary diversion of labor. It is doubtless convenient to consider the theological concern of the age as dimly pre-enlightenment; but despite the acrid quibblings of the bigoted, the ridiculous fancies of the untutored, and the tedious disquisitions of the dogmatists (all well-publicized failings of the century), an examination of the learning and Biblical research of the critics of this period reveals an over-all scholarly stature and dignity of study rarely surpassed in any era. Intellectual prestige does not rest alone upon the rise of experimental science, though, admittedly, the Royal Society is closer to our times than the *Critici Sacri*.

In discussing the work of these scholars it is necessary because of the breadth of the subject to single out names. Accordingly, it should be clear that, in so doing, an attempt is being made to cite the more notable and influential of them, solely in order to indicate the philological and critical climate of the times. Actually, as a method of selection, mention is chiefly made of those who would almost certainly have been known to Milton and whose works were extant during his life; and even with this qualification, it is necessary to omit much. For convenience of treatment (even with the inevitable overlapping) three aspects—or branches—of sacred philology will be examined, namely, the grammatical, the historical, and the exegetical.

In the first division, the work of the Buxtorfs is justly famous. Widely known for his great Rabbinical Bible,[43] Johannes Buxtorf the Elder, while professor of Hebrew at Basel, devoted himself to the study of rabbinic literature and produced up until his death in 1629 Hebraic works of such erudition and merit that, with the single exception of his judgment against Elias Levita[44] on the origin of the vowel points[45] (in his *Tiberias, sive commentarius Masoreticus*, 1620), his contributions are largely serviceable in the present day. In addition to the Rabbinical Bible he published during his life a Hebrew manual,[46] a study of Jewish ceremony full of information and lore,[47] and a lexicon;[48] but it was left to his son, Johannes, (1599–1664), to complete and publish the two works which made the elder Buxtorf's name pre-eminent among Biblical scholars: his *Lexicon Chaldaicum Talmudicum et Rabbinicum* and the *Concordantiae Bibliorum Hebraicorum*, both works of monumental industry.

The younger Buxtorf, though having achieved a right-ful place in the ranks of great scholars by the completion of his father's work, frequent editing, and the production of a lexicon for use with the Rabbinical Bible,[49] dissipated much of his time in the fruitless controversies with Cappel,[50] a formidable adversary and, unhappily for Buxtorf, completely right. The question of the antiquity of the vowel points, the subject of the main quarrel with Cappel, resulted from the conception of the infallibility of the Bible. Corollary to this idea was the belief that not only had the Bible suffered no textual alteration in its trans-mission, but that the very vowel points and accents were a result of divine inspiration.

This stand was vigorously refuted by Louis Cappel in his anonymously published *Arcanum Punctationis Rev-elatum* (1624). Cappel showed that the vowel points were added by the Massorete Jews of Tiberias in the fifth century A.D. and that the square characters of the Hebrew alphabet were substituted for an earlier Samaritan type at the time of the captivity. The younger Buxtorf in his *Tractatus de punctorum origine, antiquite et authoritate oppositus Arcano punctationis revelato Ludovici Cappelli* (1648), the refutation of Cappel, following the custom of the day (one certainly not strange to Milton), attacked Cappel's work with contempt and the usual name-calling; with what irony rests plainly in the vindication and ac-ceptance of Cappel's work by modern scholars as well as by some of the great critics of his own day.[51]

The work of Valentine Schindler[52] is not so well known. Though neither so famous nor so productive as either Buxtorf, he was the author of the first polyglot lexicon, *Lexicon Pentaglotton, Hebraicum, Chaldaicum Syriacum, Talmudico-Rabbinicum, et Arabicum* (Hanau, 1612). This is a work of no small merit and was widely used at a later period, despite the fame of the Buxtorfs. The lexicon contains considerable rabbinical material by way of illustration, in addition to specific references to commentaries of the famous rabbis, and, as will be seen, was a useful source for such information for the nonrabbinical reader.

One other lexicon of the period should be noted. This is the work of Milton's contemporary, the Puritan Edward Leigh (1602–71). The bulk of the work of this prolific writer[53] consisted of compilations and discursive rather than scholarly miscellanies; but he achieved real importance in his *Critica Sacra; or, Philologicall and Theogicall Observations upon All the Greek Words of the New Testament*, 1639, and his *Critica Sacra, Observations on All the Radices or Primitive Hebrew of the Old Testament*, 1642 both of which were published together ("in order alphabeticall") at London in 1650. This lexicon, made particularly useful by Leigh's profuse marginal quotations, somewhat in the fashion of Poole, of philological comments of numerous other exegetes, was usually a standard source for later lexicographers. Leigh's *Critica Sacra* attracted the attention of Ussher, and, as a consequence, the two became friends. There is every likelihood that Milton was acquainted with this popular work of Leigh.

Of the many studies produced in the strictly philological field in the period, most of it praiseworthy, unchallenged in eminence and unequaled in competence and learning are the books of Hottinger and Cappel.[54] The first of these authors, Johann Heinrich Hottinger (1620–67), professor of Hebrew at various times at Zurich, Heidelberg, and Leyden, was not only one of the most productive and distinguished philologists of the century but was largely instrumental in establishing firmly the method of a sound grammatical and historical foundation for interpretation of Scripture.[55] His greatest philological achievement in scriptural introduction was the *Thesaurus philologicus seu Clavis Scripturae* which appeared in 1649. This work,[56] for all its erudite quotations of Arabic, Syriac, and rabbinical originals (as necessary documentation), is a model of practicality. Complete Latin translations of the cited passages are supplied; the volume is excellently indexed (a rare thing for the times); and, while the work is manifestly intended for the scholar, the theologian of only general training could profitably make use of it.

Louis Cappel, whose controversy with Buxtorf on the vowel points has already been mentioned, was one of the greatest Hebraists of France and probably the most effective and influential philologist of Europe. His specialty was the history of the Old Testament text; and his *Critica Sacra* (Paris, 1650), a landmark in the history of linguistic science, challenged the theologically important axiom of the integrity of the Old Testament text. This reduction of the infallible Book to a problem of manuscript brought about bitter and vicious attacks but eventually—as in the case of his earlier *Arcanum Punctationem*—won general acceptance in his day and an honored place in the history of progress. Milton's remarks on the text of the Bible indicate, if not an acquaintance with Cappel, that at least he was certainly aware of the textual variants and inconsistencies, though this knowledge in no wise upset his Puritan adherence to the integrity of the doctrinal parts.[57] Cappel, of all the sacred philologists, most actively advanced the cause of the new exegesis and, in a substantial sense, marks the beginning of modern Biblical criticism.

A scholar rather than a theologian, Cappel, with his scientific historical method of procedure, must always be ranked high in the academic world.

In the broader conception of sacred philology, going beyond linguistics into history, archaeology, law, and ethnology, the scholars of the seventeenth century, with their command of Hebrew and Oriental languages, are unrivaled in sheer quantity of work. The great Scaliger[58] established the basis for chronology, Bochart[59] studied the geography and natural history of the Bible, L'Empereur[60] produced his Talmudic studies, Schickhard[61] wrote of ancient Hebrew law, and Voss[62] began the historical study of dogma. Some idea of the scope of this type of study may be gathered from Ugolino.[63]

In England this scholarship reached great heights. The names of Selden, Pococke, and Lightfoot form a triumvirate of the leading Orientalists of the age. Lightfoot (1602–75) certainly is generally recognized as the greatest of the Christian rabbinical scholars. His *Harmony of the IV Evangelists*[64] and his *Horae Hebraicae et Talmudicae*[65] are ranking studies. A great Talmud scholar (Lightfoot is usually considered the chief founder of Talmudic research in Europe),[66] he frequently used the Talmud to illustrate and explain ethnological and philological matters in the Old Testament. Lightfoot, easily England's greatest exegete, enjoyed great eminence amongst the scholars of Europe. Because of the historical competence and linguistic accuracy of his method, he follows only Cappel in furthering the development of modern technique of criticism.

Edward Pococke (1604–91) is remembered primarily as an Arabic scholar,[67] but his commentaries on some of the minor prophets reveal his stature as a Hebraist (and, incidentally, there is recorded in the Preface to these commentaries his emphasis on the translation principle of the literal meaning). His *Porta Mosis* (1655), containing portions of Maimonides's commentary on the Mishnah, was the first book to be printed in Hebrew characters at Oxford.[68] Besides his Arabic researches, he was active in the preparation of Walton's Polyglot and lent Castell Ethiopic manuscripts for the *Lexicon Heptaglotton*. Pococke was a great collector of Oriental manuscripts, some 420 of which were purchased by the Bodleian in 1693.

John Selden (1584–1654), best known today for his position in legal history (to say nothing of his pithy *Table Talk*) and deeply respected and often cited by Milton,[69] was in Oriental studies by no means the least of the three. His fame in law and letters has to a great extent obscured his position as a Hebraist. His *De Diis Syris* (1617) marks the beginning of the study of Phoenecian and Syrian mythology; and his works on Jewish law and antiquities, despite some deficiencies, display an extraordinary familiarity with rabbinical writings and contain much of permanent value. The eclectic erudition of John Selden, in an age of erudition, is to the eternal prestige of English intellectual history.

For a more immediate bearing on Milton's textual criticism of Scripture—aside from the basic grammatical and lexicographic materials—the aspect of sacred philology that is probably of most significance is that of grammatical commentaries and exegetical aids. There is implied in the first instance of grammatical commentaries the general linguistic tendency of the exegesis and its historical spirit as well as the occurrence of syntactical analysis. The grammatical exegetes were those who applied the philological approach to the scriptural text to the exclusion of mysticism or spiritual apologetics. They followed varied creeds and believed in different theological tenets; but in their attack on the Bible text, the exposition of accurate and literal meaning was their characteristic *modus operandi*, as grammar and philology were their *apparatus criticus*. Their importance lies in their assumption that theology is derived from Scripture and that, fundamentally, true theology depends upon accurate exegesis.

Cocceius and Grotius, two of the most famous and influential commentators of the age, and equal in philological competence, afford an interesting contrast in exegetical emphasis. Both were philological in method, but their attitudes and influence were markedly divergent. Cocceius,[70] although adhering absolutely to the idea that the fundamental basis of theology is Scripture, erred on the side of a somewhat typological exegesis. He used his vast learning in Greek, Hebrew, and Arabic to prove the contention that the Bible was an organic whole and that each passage should be interpreted according to the exact meaning of the words, but his tendency to derive deep meanings and his labored analogies from the plain text revived the tendency toward mystical interpretation.[71]

Sharply opposed to the Cocceian plurality of meaning or artificial delineation of deeper sense stood the exegesis of Hugo Grotius. (An epigram current in the day says it nicely: *Grotium nusquam in sacris literis invenire Christum, Cocceium ubique.*) The commentaries of Grotius, concise, analytical, and linguistic, were less theological than historical. In contrast to Cocceius, Grotius was given over entirely to rational exposition—so rational, in fact, that he was often accused of Socinianism.[72] The character of his exegesis, in addition to linguistic proficiency and rational historicity, resembled Calvin's (lacking, however, the spiritual intensity of the Great Reformer) in his uniform good judgment and what might be called exegetical tact. The commentaries of Grotius, characteristically called annotations (*Annotationes ad Veterum Testamentum*, Amsterdam, 1644), probably the most celebrated commentaries of the age in the Protestant world, were violently attacked by the splenetic Calovius[73] in his *Biblia Illustrata*, 1672, the title page of which bore the qualification "*in quibus Grotianae depravationes et ψευδερμηνεῖαι justo examine sistuntur et exploduntur*[!]." This fanatic, polemical compendium of Protestantism's "born inquisitor," when not futilely disputing Grotius's exegesis, is filled with extravagant errors; and, though rightfully forgotten today, it probably did more to increase the prestige of Grotius than the abundant contemporary encomiums attached to his name. His work, because of the stress on rational historical interpretation and, especially, because of its influence on progressive scholars,[74] is of paramount importance for the period. The historian Briggs, for one, crediting Grotius with the revival of the spirit of Erasmus, considers him the chief interpreter of the seventeenth century.[75] Milton's connection with Grotius needs no comment, and there can be no doubt that he was thoroughly familiar with the famous annotations.[76]

Of other commentators notable for linguistic emphasis (and these would include Lightfoot, Vossius, Pococke, and L'Empereur, whom we have already mentioned in connection with another type of scholarship), the exegesis of Johannes Drusius[77] was held in particular esteem by his contemporaries. Much of his work was incorporated into the *Critici Sacri*, and his minor works were reprinted late in the eighteenth century. His comparative textual study *Parallela Sacra seu comparatio locorum Vet. Text. cum eis quae in Novo citantur*, a useful and competent reference, was very well known. Drusius was a voluminous writer but produced nothing that lacked merit. Evidently, a professorship in Hebrew or Oriental languages in the seventeenth century had formidable implications, and certainly it usually involved fairly heroic results.

The *Animadversiones* (1631) of Louis de Dieu,[78] as indicated by the subtitle, *Comment. in quatuor Evangelia, in quo collatis Syri imprimio Arabii Evangelii Hebraei, Vulgati, D. Erasmi et Bezae Versionibus, difficilia loca illustrantur et variae lectiones conferuntur*, were strictly textual and grammatical in procedure. De Dieu was a remarkable scholar who typifies well the blend of Humanism and theology. He found time, despite the quantity of his other work, to write a manual of Hebrew, Syriac, and Chaldee grammar, as well as a primer of Persian, which, it must be observed, demonstrates a modicum of energy.

The greatest critical achievement in England was what can be properly described as the set of Walton's London Polyglot,[79] Castell's *Lexicon*,[80] the *Critici Sacri*,[81] and Matthew Poole's *Synopsis*,[82] twenty-two huge folios forming in themselves a nearly complete exegetical library. Begun and finished in the space of twenty-three years (1653–76), these great tomes are a landmark of national co-operative scholarship. Of either their magnitude or fame it is not necessary to speak. Milton's direct use of them (all appeared after his blindness) is problematical, but he must have known with pride of their existence.[83]

Most familiar to him of the critical labors of his countrymen we should expect to find the works of Hammond,

Mead, Lightfoot, and such Puritans as Gataker, Weemse, Cartwright, Ainsworth, Goodwin, and Leigh. Two of these (probably the least known today), while not remarkable as theologians nor especially notable politically, enjoyed considerable contemporary prestige.

Thomas Gataker (1574–1654), mentioned by Milton,[84] is of particular interest. In refutation of *Diatribe de linguae graecae N. Testamenti puritate* of Sebastian Pfocken (in which the purity of the Greek text of the New Testament was laboriously maintained against those who suggested the presence of Hebraisms),[85] Gataker wrote his *De Novi Instrumenti Stylo Dissertatio* (1648), one of the most brilliant philological essays of the age. By a searching study of comparative linguistics which displayed a powerful grasp of Hebrew and Greek and which was illustrated by a mass of quotations from classical Greek writings,[86] Gataker irrefutably proved the existence of Hebraisms in the New Testament. He was a member of the Westminster Assembly and one of the committee of seven who prepared the first draft of the Confession of Faith.

The works of John Weemse (*ca.*1579–1636) were highly praised and widely read by his contemporaries. His best known book, the *Christian Synagogue*,[87] reached a fourth edition within ten years of publication. Weemse's writing, though more popular in approach (the *Christian Synagogue* was written in English) and less erudite in content than those we have been discussing, was highly competent. That he reached a large audience was due, not only to his expository style, but also to the enthusiasm and interest of even the mildly educated for the new Biblical learning.[88]

We have summarily surveyed the growth and scope of sacred philology in order to indicate the nature of the new exegetical school of which Milton was a part. Men of disparate faiths, it has been plain, followed the principle of literal interpretation; the sacred philologists represented no cult but rather shared the same attitude toward Biblical criticism. The application of the linguistic technique in exegesis varied naturally with the doctrinal axioms of specific creeds, but common to the movement as a whole was the belief that understanding of all things divine rested upon analysis of the original scriptural text. The radical tendencies of philology could scarcely develop under the disciplined supervision of the Roman Church; and it is, therefore, chiefly amongst the Protestants that the extremes of doctrinal derivation resulted from the manifold variants of translation. Even at the height of the movement, some conservative Protestants became suspicious of the exegetical dogmatizing which seemed invariably to lead to the company of Socinus;[89] and, indeed, by the end of the seventeenth century, philology, though not losing its critical importance, was relegated to the status of an adjacent study.

In the great corpus of grammatical data and analyses of the difficult passages of both the Old and New Testaments produced by the philologists, there was available to the Puritan peruser of Scripture all the material necessary for the discovery of the true and final sense of Scripture. For him, the theological deductions of a commentator were not necessarily important so long as the literal meaning of the original had been established; but given this accuracy of text and the infallible guidance of the Holy Spirit, the truth of doctrine must inevitably follow. It is pertinent, then, to observe that the whole critical learning of the age was at Milton's disposal. To what extent he used specific commentators or treatises may never be fully known. It is manifest, however, that he was not only aware of the existence of such material, but, intellectually and spiritually bound as he was by his hermeneutics to seek sedulously the plain word of God, it was impossible for him not to have consulted at large in it.

This proposition can be made clear by examining the formulation of Milton's theory of Scripture and his principle of interpretation.

II

Hermeneutics

From the reformation hermeneutics of Martin Luther, whose chief tenet was Scripture above ecclesiastical authority and whose principle of scriptural interpretation by Scripture advanced Biblical supremacy in all matters of doctrine, came the basic Protestant theory of the absolute sufficiency of Scripture in Christian theology. The extreme practice of this tenet is to be found amongst the later Puritans, but it was definitively set forth in the Westminster Confession[1] and most ably propounded earlier by the Anglican, William Chillingworth.

The rational tolerance of Chillingworth,[2] though a far cry from the rigorous dogmatism of the conservative Independents, in the exposition of his famous rebuttal to Knott's axiom of the Church's infallible voice, evolved the dictum that all Protestantism followed generally and the Puritans specifically; that is (in his often paraphrased words), "The Bible, I say, the Bible only, is the religion of Protestants."[3] But it is in Chillingworth's delineation of the scriptural rule of faith that we find the best expression of those principles of interpretation which were the foundation of Milton's *De Doctrina.* Most significant of these principles, and the instance where Chillingworth is clearly apart from either Anglican or conservative Puritan, is his insistence on the free right of individual interpretation of Scripture, with its obvious corollary of latitude in the minor conclusions therefrom. As against:

This presumptuous imposing of the senses of men upon the words of God, the special senses of men upon the general words of God, and laying them upon men's consciences together, under the penalty of death and damnation; this vain conceit that we can speak of the things of God better than in the words of God; this deifying our own interpretations, and tyrannous enforcing them upon others,[4]

Chillingworth advances the idea of individual exegesis:

All we say is this—that we have reason to believe that God *de facto*, hath ordered the matter so, that all the Gospel of Christ, the whole covenant between God and man is now written . . . . the scripture is not a judge of controversies, but a rule only, and the only rule, for Christians to judge them by. Every man is to judge for himself with the judgment of discretion . . . . For if the scripture (as it is in things necessary) be plain, why should it be more necessary to have a judge to interpret the meaning of a council's decrees, and others to interpret their interpretations, and others to interpret theirs, and so on forever. And where they are not plain, there if we, using diligence to find the truth, do yet miss of it and fall into error, there is no danger. They that err, and they that do not err, may both be saved.[5]

From this premise Chillingworth advances, in a magnificent passage, the proposition of freedom of religious opinion:

In a word, there is no sufficient certainty but of scripture only for any considering man to build upon. This, therefore, and this only, I have reason to believe: this I will profess, according to this I will live, and for this, if there be occasion, I will not only willingly, but even gladly, lose my life, though I should be sorry that Christians should take it from me. Propose me any thing out of this book, and require whether I believe it or no, and seem it never so incomprehensible to human reason, I will subscribe it with hand and heart, as knowing no demonstration can be stronger than this; God hath said so, therefore it is true. In other things I will take no man's liberty of judgment from him; neither shall any man take mine from me. I will think no man the worse man, nor the worse Christian, I will love no man the less, for differing in opinion from me. And what measure I mete to others, I expect from them again. I am fully assured that God does not, and therefore that men ought not to require any more of any man than this, to believe the scripture to be God's word, to endeavor to find the true sense of it, and to live according to it.[6]

Significant, here, is Chillingworth's conception of belief in the irrational, the things "incomprehensible to human reason." Because of Milton's identical position it is important to understand that this in no way opens the door to mystic or fanciful interpretation. The word of God is final and may at times transcend comprehension, but the "judgment of discretion" through which the rule of Scripture is manifested is a wholly rational process.[7] In answering his opponent's argument that if papal infallibility were eliminated, every man would be given over to his own wit and discourse, Chillingworth retorts:

If you mean by *discourse* right reason grounded on divine revelation, and common notions written by God in the hearts of all men, and deducing, according to the never-failing rules of logic consequent deductions from them;—if this be it which you mean by discourse, it is very meet and reasonable and necessary that men . . . . should be left unto it; and he that follows this in all his opinions and actions follows always God.[8]

He goes on to say that God cannot accept the sacrifice of fools; and, therefore, even with divine guidance, reason plays the active role. Private interpretation is not the mere persuasion that a doctrine is true because it comes direct from the Spirit of God, but is a rational judgment dependent on evidence.[9] He then asks:

For is there not a manifest difference between saying, "The spirit of God tells me that this is the meaning of such a text," (which no man can possibly know to be true, it being a secret thing), and between saying, "These and these reasons I have to shew that this or that is true doctrine, or that this or that is the meaning of such a scripture?" Reason being a public and certain thing, and exposed to all men's trial and examination.[10]

Chillingworth strongly insists too on the essential simplicity of Scripture;[11] and in these three principles: freedom of interpretation, reason under Divine Guidance, and plainness of text, we can, except for the lesser eloquence of the *De Doctrina*, hear Milton speaking. There are, to be sure, other points of similarity between them;[12] but in these main tenets of *The Religion of Protestants* we have the complete basis for Milton's hermeneutics.

Puritan expression of these principles is less lofty and somewhat militant,[13] but it is significant to note their emphasis on literal exactness as against the more general Chillingworth conception of free interpretation. Noteworthy, too, is the authoritative position assigned to the Hebrew and Greek original. John Ball sums up the Puritan position concisely:

The means to find out the true meaning of the Scripture, are conference of one place of Scripture with another, diligent consideration of the scope and circumstances of the place, as the occasions, and coherence of that which went before, with that which followeth after; the matter whereof it doth intreat, and circumstances of persons, times and places, and consideration, whether the words are spoken figuratively or simply; for in figurative speeches, not the outward shew of words, but the sense is to be taken and knowledge of the arts and tongues wherein the Scriptures were originally written.[14]

The iteration of this method of interpretation, the fundamental rationale of their scriptural theology, naturally abounds in Puritan writings. Almost all the systems of divinity compiled by them include some sort of paraphrase of the ideas set down by Ball. On the matter of deference to the Hebrew and Greek, though not insisting upon the original version for normal Christian practice, John Goodwin in his *Divine Authority of the Scriptures Asserted* (London, 1648) is especially eloquent:

Though I judge no translation whatsoever, either for gracefull-nesse of language, significancie of terms, majesty of expression (with the like) to be equall to the Originall Hebrew and Greek; yet I conceive that there is no translation so farre degenerate or so disadvantagiously compil'd, but that carrieth θεῖον τι, something differing by way of excellencie from the manner of men, in the phrase and language thereof; yea, that which is sufficient, by the ordinary blessing of God upon a consciencious and intent reading, or consideration of it, to evince the descent of the matter contained in it, to be from God, as a seal of armes upon the outside of a letter, is sufficient to discover from what person of honour the matter or contents of the letter come.[15]

Goodwin, like Chillingworth, sees Scripture open to all men and, accordingly, cannot insist upon the sole accuracy of learned interpretation of the original.

The distinction was frequently made by the Puritans between the "special and peculiar" rules of Bible reading for scholars and "the more general and common direction for Christians of all sort, learned and unlearned."[16] Since Milton is in the former class it is interesting to see what the renowned John Owen[17] has to say of the means for interpretation of Scripture through the original, under the method he terms the "disciplinarian":

That which of this sort I prefer in the first place is the knowledge of, and skill in the languages wherein the Scripture was orig-inally written . . . . It must be acknowledged that the Scripture as written in these languages, is accompanied with many and great advantages. (1). In them peculiarly is it γραφὴ θεόπνευστος, a writing by divine inspiration, 2 Tim. iii 16. And ספר יהוה the book of the writings of the Lord, Isa. xxxiv. 16. with a singular privilege above all translation . . . . The sacred sense indeed of the words and expression is the *Internum formale sacrum*, or that wherein the holiness of the Scripture doth consist. But the writing itself in the original languages, in the words chosen and used by the Holy Ghost, is the *externum formale*, of the Holy Scripture, and is materially sacred . . . . There is in the originals of the Scripture a peculiar emphasis of words and expressions, and in them an especial energy to intimate and insinuate the sense of the Holy Ghost into the minds of men, which cannot be traduced into other languages by translation, so as to obtain the same power and efficacy.[18]

Owen goes on at great length to demonstrate the necessity of skill and knowledge of the original for those who are called unto the interpretation of Scripture in order to guide others less gifted in languages. But in so doing he warns (completely paralleling Milton's attitude) of the dangers of "noisome elations of mind" and the vanity of overannotation for "this skill and faculty where it hath been unaccompanied with that humility, sobriety, reverence of the author of the Scripture, and respect unto the analogy of faith, which ought to bear sway in the minds of all men who undertake to expound the oracles of God, may be, and hath been greatly abused unto the hurt of its owners, and disadvantages of the church."[19] Noxious and profane curiosity causes the growth of fruitless conjectures as vain for the most part as those of the cabalistical Jews. "And this humour," concludes Owen (as did Milton with almost the same words), "hath filled us with needless and futilous observations, which, beyond an ostentation of the learning of their authors (indeed the utmost end whereunto they are designed) are of no use nor consideration."[20] Learning and skill in Hebrew and Greek by all means but only when accompanied by humility of spirit and utter dependence on the Holy Ghost.

Owen's whole treatment of scriptural interpretation and method of criticism, too extensive to quote further, is one of the best, if not the most elaborate, of all statements of Puritan hermeneutics. Milton's exposition of the same topic might be fairly described as a synopsis of the disciplines of John Owen. In order to compare Milton's system of Biblical criticism with the Protestant-Puritan philological theory of his day, it is convenient to enumerate here (omitting such commonplaces as the canon, the idea of Scripture for all, and the usual illustrative passages from the Bible) the principle tenets we have noticed so far as a reference point for an examination of Milton's system. The following principles appear to be basic: Scripture alone for salvation; reason under the guidance of the Holy Ghost for understanding of the text; plainness and simplicity of the Bible; importance of consulting the original Hebrew and Greek; free interpretation and humble integrity of exegesis. These we should find to be the beliefs of John Milton.

The doctrine of Scripture alone is the cardinal tenet of Milton's hermeneutics; his whole theology is directly dependent upon it. Eternal salvation, argues Milton, is granted by God only through the faith of the individual. Therefore, in the very opening of the *De Doctrina*, the necessary procedure of his treatise is set down:

But since it is only to the individual faith of each that the Deity has opened the way of eternal salvation, and as he requires that he who would be saved should have a personal belief of his own, I resolved not to repose on the faith or judgment of others in matters relating to God; but on the one hand, having taken the grounds of my faith from divine revelation alone, and on the other, having neglected nothing which depended on my own industry, I thought fit to scrutinize and ascertain for myself the several points of my religious belief, by the most careful perusal and meditation of the Holy Scriptures themselves.[21]

Divine revelation alone by perusal of Scripture, dependent upon neither the faith nor judgment of any other is the axiom of method. Thus his acknowledgment of the study of a few of the shorter systems of divines and consultation of larger theological treatises must be carefully qualified. Milton's explanation is characteristically blunt:

I entered upon an assiduous course of study in my youth, beginning with the books of the Old and New Testament in their original languages, and going diligently through a few of the shorter systems of divines, in imitation of whom I was in the habit of classing under certain heads whatever passages of Scripture occurred for extraction, to be made use of hereafter as occasion might require. At length I resorted with increased confidence to some of the more copious theological treatises, and to the examination of the arguments advanced by the conflicting parties respecting certain disputed points of faith. But, to speak the truth with freedom as well as candor, I was concerned to discover in many instances adverse reasonings either evaded by wretched shifts, or attempted to be refuted, rather speciously than with solidity, by an affected display of formal sophisms, or by a constant recourse to the quibbles of the grammarians .... According to my judgment, therefore, neither my creed nor my hope of salvation could be safely trusted to such guides .... I deemed it therefore safest and most advisable to compile for myself, by my own labor and study, some original treatise which should be always at hand, derived solely from the word of God itself, and executed with all possible fidelity, seeing that I could have no wish to practice any imposition on myself in such a matter.[22]

The shorter systems merely suggested the structure and form, while the consultation of the larger theological treatises proved by their grammatical quibblings and specious sophistries that neither creed nor salvation could be based upon them. In preparation for this original treatise derived solely from the word of God itself (*solo Dei verbo*), Milton admits to years of study and constant diligence in his unwearied search after truth. Finally, he sums up his absolute independence and integrity of purpose by pointing out that he had not read the heterodoxical works until the critical blunders of the orthodox inclined him to the occasionally superior exegesis of the so-called "heretics" and emphatically reaffirms his adherence to Holy Scripture alone:

> For my own part, I adhere to the Holy Scriptures alone; I follow no other heresy or sect. I had not even read any of the works of heretics, so called, when the mistakes of those who are reckoned for orthodox, and their incautious handling of Scripture, first taught me to agree with their opponents whenever those opponents agreed with Scripture.[23]

In his later chapter on the Holy Scriptures,[24] a more formal treatment of the Scripture alone principle is given (and there are, besides, copious allusions to Biblical sufficiency in his prose works and one at least in *Paradise Lost*);[25] but the passages cited contain Milton's strongest expression of the idea.

What must be particularly noticed in Milton's treatment of this fundamental basis of purely scriptural theology is his insistence on absolute independence and originality. This insistence on Milton's part, it is of highest importance to understand, was not simply a matter of the undesirability of dependence on human authority. On the contrary, to Milton, any dependency but to Scripture alone under Divine guidance was expressly forbidden;[26] for, indeed, such a procedure would impose a yoke on the Holy Spirit itself:

Hence it follows, that when an acquiescence in human opinions or an obedience to human authority in matters of religion is exacted, in the name either of the church or of the Christian magistrate, from those who are themselves led individually by the Spirit of God, this is in effect to impose a yoke, not on man, but on the Holy Spirit itself.[27]

Further, Milton's whole conception of divine revelation is dependent on the Scripture alone thesis. Christian doctrine, Milton argues, is the divine revelation disclosed by Christ concerning the nature and worship of God for the promotion of God's glory and the salvation of man.[28] And, Milton concludes, this divine revelation can only be obtained from the Bible alone by means of the guidance of the Holy Spirit: "This doctrine, therefore, is to be obtained, not from the schools of the philosophers, nor from the laws of man, but from the Holy Scriptures alone, under the guidance of the Holy Spirit."[29]

Not from the philosophers, not from the laws of men, but from the Bible. We are dealing with no forensic attitudes in this independent search for God's truth; the sufficiency of Scripture and the necessity for individual interpretation unfettered by human judgments are axioms of Milton's system. Whatever there may be in the way of the residue of subconscious borrowings either from the rabbis or contemporary theologians, as suggested by Harris Fletcher,[30] there is no *de facto* reason to doubt Milton's repeated affirmation of originality, especially since originality and free, private interpretation, were for him matters of theological necessity and not rhetorical choice. The matter of Milton's borrowing in *Paradise Lost*, his wholesale use of classical figures of speech and the marked influence of contemporary poets, obviously is an entirely unrelated problem. The *De Doctrina* is not a literary work; it is Milton's solemn and private confession of faith. Milton's independence of interpretation, purely theological, does not, naturally, eliminate dependence on the grammatical tools for Biblical criticism. Whatever was necessary for the diligent searching out of the true doctrine from the pure original of God's word (*perpetuae diligentiae verique reperiendi indefesso studio, non credulitati supinae proposita esse a Deo etiam in religione omnia, tum facile perspexi*)[31] was part of the Lord's intention. We shall see, as a matter of fact, that Milton frequently agrees with the grammatical analyses of scriptural passages by various theologians, while completely disregarding their doctrinal conclusions.

Milton frequently comments on the plain sense and simplicity of the Holy Scriptures. This dictum appears frequently in his tracts, stated usually as a contrast and rebuke to the sophisms and quibbles of theologians. In the *De Doctrina*, however, it is treated as the great truth that in all things necessary to salvation, Scripture is clear. Thus:

The Scriptures, therefore, partly by reason of their own simplicity, and partly through the divine illumination, are plain and perspicuous in all things necessary to salvation, and adapted to the instruction even of the most unlearned, through the medium of diligent and constant reading.[32]

But even in this chapter of the *De Doctrina*, Milton deplores the useless technicalities and metaphysical intricacies of the Protestant divines ("through what infatuation is it, that even Protestant divines persist in darkening the most momentous truths of religion by intricate metaphysical comments"[33]). Only those who perish, he concludes, find obscurity in Scripture.

While the plain Scripture is adapted for the daily reading of all classes and orders of men,[34] Milton's exegetical requisites for scholarly and professional interpretation reflect perfectly the new philology. Actually, they are not only a summary of the best philological principles evolved in his day, but they want nothing for the guidance of a modern exegete. The logician and grammarian in Milton are strikingly evident here:

> The requisites for the public interpretation of Scripture have been laid down by divines with much attention to usefulness, although they have not been observed with equal fidelity. They consist in knowledge of languages; inspection of the originals; examination of the context; care in distinguishing between literal and figurative expressions; consideration of cause and circumstance, of antecedents and consequents; mutual comparison of texts; and regard to the analogy of faith. Attention must also be paid to the frequent anomalies of syntax.... Lastly, no inferences from the text are to be admitted, but such as follow necessarily and plainly from the words themselves.[35]

This is surely a précis of scholarly method: knowledge of languages, inspection of the original text, examination of context, distinction between literal and figurative language, regard for anomalies of syntax, comparison of text, consideration of cause and circumstance, and no textual inferences beyond those that follow necessarily from the actual words of the passage. A Bentley could say no more.

As for the integrity of the Biblical text, Milton demonstrates his familiarity with the problems of variant readings and spurious passages[36] of Scripture known at the time. He avoids both the near mystic compromises of the Cocceians and the jot-and-tittle stubbornness of the unreasoning dogmatists. That there are corruptions of text, not to mention spurious books, Milton does not deny:

> For the external Scripture, or written word, particularly of the New Testament, to say nothing of spurious books .... the written word, I say, of the New Testament, has been liable to frequent corruption, and in some instances has been corrupted,

through the number, and occasionally the bad faith of those by whom it has been handed down, the variety and discrepancy of the original manuscripts, and the additional diversity produced by subsequent transcripts and printed editions.[37]

He recognizes too that the historical books of the Old Testament are of uncertain authorship and that there are contradictions on points of chronology; but he hastens to add that this in no way destroys the integrity of their doctrinal parts.[38] He conjectures what the purpose of Providence could be in committing the writings to such uncertain guardianship and decides that the purpose must be to teach reliance on the Holy Spirit. This tack, in the face of the difficulty, Milton adopts for resolution of the problem. The process of belief for Milton becomes mainly a reaffirmation of dependency on the Holy Spirit coupled with the internal evidence implied in the general tenor of the whole of Scripture.[39]

Milton's conception of the role of reason in exegesis, and its relation to divine guidance, has been, perhaps justifiably, somewhat misunderstood because of his statement (made in the intricate chapter on the Son) that we should discard reason in sacred things and follow the Scriptures exclusively (*Nos itaque in sacris rationi renuntiemus; quod divina scriptura docet, id unice sequamur*).[40] There is certainly no need, however, as in the case of the Anglican historian, John Hunt,[41] sarcastically to parade with inane literalism Milton's supposed inconsistency as evidence of his total incompetence in theology. In the first place, there is nothing inconsistent in Milton's apparent disavowal of reason, as is plain from even a careless reading of the passage in which it occurs. What Milton is really advocating is nothing more than to refrain from reasoning on things of mystery, an utterance as old as Aeschylus. Milton's statement follows a rather long disquisition on the problem of ens, essence, duality, and all the difficult terminological paraphernalia of the nature of the Son; his conclusion to accept imponderables and to depend solely on the Holy Ghost is a convenient solution to a fruitless speculation. Certainly it does not mean to give up the use of reason by which Milton believed God intended men to seek freely from Scripture his saving word; *ratio* as used in this phrase means not a faculty of the mind, but argumentation or production of proof, a common usage (as any lexicon will confirm). For the larger question of rationalistic exegesis in the sixteenth and seventeenth century, the Socinian movement is of first importance.

Of all the religious groups of the period, the Socinians through their exegesis come closest to the specific heresies of Milton. Further, though basically different in theological doctrine, and while advancing the status and function of reason beyond all theological decorum,[42] the Socinian spirit of rational foundation in religion and their exegetical, logical, and direct deductions from Scripture (even without the Holy Ghost of the *De Doctrina*) are thoroughly in accord with Milton's practice. In a large sense, and especially as the term was used in seventeenth-century polemics as an opprobrious epithet (almost invariably hurled at superior exegetes and reminiscent in fact of the old connotation of liberal), Socinianism is less a corpus of doctrine than an attitude toward religious enquiry. Inspiration was limited by the Socinians to things essential, and slight errors were acknowledged in things unessential.[43]

In terms of scriptural derivation, the Racovian Catechism[44] has the same genesis as Milton's *De Doctrina*. This remarkable work, though often formally refuted, had considerable influence in Germany, Holland, and England,

and may, as maintained by a recent historian of the movement, have modified the letter and spirit of Protestant theology.[45]

The Socinian confession of faith (which is actually what the Racovian Catechism amounts to), unlike the existing Protestant confessions which were formulated by professional theologians who supported a generally traditional and organized scheme of doctrine from texts of Scripture, was begun by Socinus (who had no professional theological training), completely independent of tradition and pointedly disavowing existing creeds, by direct deduction from Scripture. Trained in legal reasoning, Socinus approached Scripture (as Wilbur phrases it)[46] "as to a *corpus juris*"; the resultant system, instead of being centered in faith, is based on the attainment of salvation through divinely revealed and logically proved evidence. Whatever the doctrinal extremes and overemphasis of reason that characterized the followers of the Racovian school, the Socinians, along with some Arminians (especially such as Episcopius),[47] served as a healthy counterirritant to the growing and opposing groups of mystical interpreters, who either partially or wholly[48] forsook the literal sense and, accordingly, weakened the whole grammatico-historical method.

As against the Socinians, Milton was unswerving in his adherence to the fundamental formula of divine guidance; he was too sound a Puritan to do otherwise; but he was, on the other hand, with the rationalists, completely devoid of mystical tendencies. Divine guidance in Milton's system insures the truth; but with that security, God requires diligence and understanding in seeking out salvation.[49] Milton's criticism of the Bible is comparable to the Socinian in attack and coincidental in exegetically evolved heresies.

Because of his appreciation of the philological scholarship of the age, Milton, like his friend Grotius, was not guilty of the narrow literalism of the Calovian type. However deficient his doctrinal conclusions from the standpoint of formal Christian theologies (or in a lesser sense from mere orthodoxy), Milton's theory and practice of Biblical interpretation, founded so solidly upon the classic Protestant hypothesis of scriptural sufficiency, can be regarded as superior to the main extravagances of the period. Neither circumscribed by bibliolatry, on the one hand, nor, on the other, limited by mystical intuition, Milton, utilizing the scholarly works available to him, and with utmost solemnity of purpose, formulated his system of Christian doctrine, the Milton confession, upon his energetic and conscientious study of the Bible. The humility with which he advanced his ideas[50] and the importance he assigned to the work (his "best and richest possession")[51] remove the *Christian Doctrine* from the category of a tract or mere exercise. We may disagree with Milton's evaluation of the treatise, but we are obliged to acknowledge its originality. Ames and Wolleb may have suggested its structure (they would surely have deplored its contents); there may be inherent in such a work subconscious indebtedness to others, and doubtless the Puritan world in which he lived suggested many of its tangents, but the only collaborator acknowledged by its author is the Holy Spirit.

Historical evidence for Milton's claim of solitary authorship will be presented in the last two chapters. At this point it is at least clear that Milton's theory of interpretation was Puritan and his exegetical method admittedly philological. Certainly for Milton, *Regula itaque fidei et canon, scriptura sola est.*[52]

Before inspecting the actual practice of his exegesis, there remain the matter of his own linguistic ability for purposes of Biblical criticism and the question of his specific indebtness to rabbinical exegesis. The first, if our understanding of Milton's criticism is correct, should indicate a high degree of nonspecialized competence; and the second, the theory of rabbinical influence on the formulation of his own theological conceptions, should be groundless.

III

Milton's Linguistic Equipment

THE REPUTATION of Cromwell's Latin secretary as a linguist scarcely needs amplification; this facet of Humanism Milton possessed to an almost heroic degree. Masson's estimate of Milton's Latinity has never been challenged;[1] and Milton's whole scheme of language study, as reported by Phillips,[2] is still a matter for some awe. But an estimate of the degree of learning reached by Milton in Hebrew and Greek for the purpose of textual criticism of Scripture needs qualification. The importance of seeking out God's Word in "the originall tongues" was vital to Milton's hermeneutics. For the Puritan especially, sacred philology involved, by definition, a far more solemn orientation and exactness of study than the ordinary acquisition of proficiency in the ancient languages for the study of profane letters. God was no muse. The purpose of learning the languages of the Bible was for the singular and paramount function of exact rendition of the text and establishment of the true sense of Scripture. Nor was it simply a question of theological erudition; rather what was at stake was salvation itself or, in the militant clichés of the day, the rescue of man from the errors of Popery. Although Masson observed that there is little in the way of results by which we can test Milton's knowledge of Greek and Hebrew, he does admit that "there is evidence of his acquaintance with Greek authors and of his having more than ventured on Hebrew."[3]

The problem of Milton's abilities in Greek, considering the normal university practices of the times[4] and Milton's own classicism, need not detain us. The evidence to which Masson alludes, Milton's own copy of Aratus with critical marginalia and textual notes in his own hand, does, however, take on some significance when examined by the great historian of classical scholarship. Sandys[5] remarks that the marginal memoranda in Milton's annotated copies of Pindar, Euripides, Lycophron, and Aratus proved that Milton read the Greek poets with the eye of a critic. He then goes on to say, by way of an estimate of Milton's Greek, that "his reading was that of a poet and general scholar rather than that of a professional philologer."[6] So ranks Milton in the history of Greek scholars according to the not inconsiderable judgment of Sandys.

This aspect of his status in Greek is precisely the point that must be made of Milton's knowledge of Hebrew. If Milton, the general scholar, was no Scaliger or Lipsius in Greek, even less was he a Lightfoot or Cappel in Hebrew. In Hebrew especially, considering what was implied by the term in the seventeenth century, he was no professional philologist. So far as exegesis is concerned, the only thing of consequence is that he knew enough Greek and Hebrew to read with ease the Biblical original and certainly enough to make intelligent and proficient use of the works of the professional philologists available. To say more than this, as in the case of the rabbinical readings, is speculation. Detailed analysis of some of Milton's exegesis will be made later; but before considering his equipment in Hebrew, there is one example of his textual criticism of New Testament Greek that should be noticed here since it not only affords us a good instance of Milton's linguistic technique but also may throw some light on the possible identity of the exegetes whom, in the passage concerned, Milton considered as interpreters of sagacity (*interpretes sagaciores*).

This occurs in the reference in the *De Doctrina* to Acts 13:48[7] where Milton advances the proper translation of the participle of τάσσω. In refutation of predestination, the subject of the chapter, he is making the point that a man is ordained to eternal life because he will believe, not that a man believes because he is ordained.[8] How could anyone be worthy before the Gospel had been preached unless on account of his being ordained (*ordinatus*), that is (he defines), well inclined or disposed to eternal life?[9] Observing that the usual translation of τεταγμένοι as *ordinati* is not justifiable, Milton argues (as uniformly shown in the clearest manner by Scripture—*cum tota scriptura manifestissimum sit*):

For these reasons other interpreters of more sagacity, according to my judgment, have thought that there is some ambiguity in the Greek word which is translated "ordained," and that it has the same force as "well or moderately disposed or affected," of a composed, attentive, upright, and not disorderly mind; of a different spirit from those Jews, as touching eternal life, who had put from them the word of God, and had shown themselves unworthy of everlasting life. The Greeks use the word in a similar sense, as in Plutarch.[10]

That the interpreters of more sagacity agreed with Milton's belief in the manifest clarity of Scripture as to the correct rendition is demonstrated by the exegetical frequency of Milton's analysis. Of course, in view of the doctrine concerned, it is not surprising to see that Calvin, Beza, and others of their school insist on *ordinati*; but it is interesting to observe that among the exegetes on Milton's side are Grotius,[11] Hammond,[12] Mead, as well as Socinus the Elder. The founder of Socinianism in his *Praelectiones Theologicae* translates τεταγμένοι in the same way as Milton:

"Verbum enim *ordinati sunt*, ita accipi potest, ut accommodationem et aptitudinem quandam a nemine factam, sed ex re ipsa provenientem declaret, perinde ac si dictum fuisset, Apti atque accommodati erant."[13] And in the Racovian Catechism the same reading is advanced specifically to refute the doctrine of predestination.[14]

Because of the position of Joseph Mead as tutor at Christ's College during Milton's residence at Cambridge, and the obvious plausibility of Milton's likely acquaintance with his work,[15] the remarks of Mead on the passage, strikingly close to the substance of Milton's,[16] are of particular interest. Mead has:

"v.48 [Acts 13] that is, the Σεβόμενοι [proselytes], who were already *in procinctu*, and *in the posture to eternal life* . . . . This I take to be the true and genuine meaning of this passage . . . . The use of the word τάσσω, de acie et collocatione militum, de ascriptione in ordinem vel classem, as it relates to an army, the disposing or marshalling of souldiers, the being listed or enrolled into such a rank or company, (in which signification the Passive is most frequent,) is well enough known. According to which sense and notion, the words might be rendered, *Crediderunt quotquot nomina sua dederant vitae aeternae*; or, (*per Ellipsin Participii*) *qui de agmine et classe fuerant sperantium vel contendentium ad vitam aeternam*; otherwise *qui in procinctu stabant ad vitam aeternam*; or most fitly, (*sensu modo militari, non destinationis,*) *quotquot ordinati fuerant ad vitam aeternam*. The sense whereof is in brief this; *They believed as many as had listed themselves*, or, *were of the company of those that did hope or earnestly labour for eternal life*, or *were in a ready posture and disposed to* or *for eternal life. De re tota judicent viri doci*"[17]

What is interesting (besides the delightfully donnish exercise in translation) in Mead's exposition is his adherence to the usual classic definition and his extension of the military denotation (the first meaning in lexicons) of τάσσω. In his marginalia to the commentary, it should be added, is a reference to Plutarch's usage. For purely linguistic authority (other than exegetical) in support of Milton's conclusion it is sufficient to record that both the Budé and Estienne lexicons, the most famous of the period, list under "τεταγμένος," *compositus, non dissolutus,* and both, like Milton, cite Plutarch as an example of this rendition.[18]

Now while there was a broader function to the study of Greek, inasmuch as classical philosophy, rhetoric, and literature were normally part of the university curriculum of the age, there was only one purpose for the study of Hebrew, namely, to read Scripture. For Milton, in fact, this was the necessity for knowing Hebrew.[19] What constituted the normal training in Hebrew for the period is well enough known,[20] and Milton unquestionably received thorough training in Biblical Hebrew. That is to say, Milton specifically studied the Hebrew Bible, doubtless comparing readings from the Septuagint, consulting lexicons and grammars for his own translation, and principally developing a great familiarity with the passages of the Hebrew version. But the dichotomy between the competent reader of Biblical Hebrew and the learned scholar of Hebraica was, in terms of training and erudition, rather profound. Years of concentrated study and, as a rule, tutoring by Jewish masters,[21] after the foundation of Biblical Hebrew had been acquired, were necessary in order to probe into the various rabbinical texts and manuscripts then available.[22] The transition from a pointed to an unpointed Hebrew Bible would cause little difficulty to Milton, but to go into the peculiar unpointed script and idiom of the extra-Biblical rabbinic writings would have involved the same sort of study as engaged the Christian Hebraists. But there was actually no need in view of the considerable amount of rabbinical Hebrew in Latin translation[23] for

Milton to have pursued such a study; and from the actual Hebrew references in his works, there is no evidence of a specialized knowledge of rabbinic Hebrew.

The best available evidence in Milton's works by which to gauge his knowledge of Hebrew is to be found in the *Nine Psalms Done into English Meter*,[24] the only Hebrew exercise, so to speak, that Milton has left us. This translation, whatever its poetic merits, does indicate that Milton read the pointed Hebrew of the Psalms with painstaking precision.[25] Inserted in the margins of Psalms LXX, LXXXI, LXXXII, and LXXXIII are Milton's transliterations of some words of the original Hebrew text. These are so extraordinarily accurate that no less a scholar than Israel Abrahams[26] has mentioned them as evidence of Milton's remarkable understanding of the vowel points. Nor is Abrahams the only Hebrew scholar who has commented upon Milton's Hebrew. Professor Gerhard,[27] commenting on Harris Fletcher's conjecture that the amanuensis laboriously copied the Hebrew words cited in the *De Doctrina* directly from a Hebrew Bible, has shown that from the evidence of numerous mistakes in the citation of Hebrew words and various errors in the pointing (such as the omission of the dagesh in ‫ב‬ in ‫בְּרָא‬) that it is, on the contrary, very evident that the copyist did not transcribe directly from a copy of the Scriptures in Hebrew. There is, Professor Gerhard feels, a strong possibility that the words were either copied from imperfect notes or else from Milton's dictation. Because a number of the Latin Biblical quotations strongly suggest that Milton often quoted from memory, there is a strong likelihood that Milton also knew the Hebrew text sufficiently well to quote it. In any case, both the evidence of the translation of the Psalms and the infrequent occurrence of Hebrew words in the *De Doctrina*, while shedding light on Milton's use of pointed Biblical Hebrew, in no way point toward rabbinical readings.

Two examples of Milton's literal lexicographic attack on Hebrew may demonstrate the possibility that his own faithful translations rather than more recondite esoterica may be a good Milton source. Both of these originate from Scripture—from the literal Hebrew of Scripture—and both have been treated as extra-Biblical embellishments or parallels to ideas in *Paradise Lost*. The first, described as a noteworthy and obvious deviation from Scripture on Milton's part (and one which, in Mr. Fletcher's opinion, has never been adequately explained),[28] occurs in Milton's treatment of a passage from the Book of Proverbs.[29] The deviation in question is Milton's use of the word "compasses" as the name of what the Creator laid upon the face of the deep instead of the more literal "circle" of the Hebrew text. Milton has written:

> and in his hand
> He took the golden Compasses, prepar'd
> In God's Eternal store, to circumscribe
> This Universe, and all created things:
> One foot he center'd and the other turn'd
> Round through the vast profunditie obscure,[30]

Mr. Fletcher feels that Milton's employment of the word "compasses" leads to the curious dilemma of finding Milton's Hebrew at fault. Curious, indeed, since the logical justification for Milton's usage occurs in the Authorized Version, which reads, "when he set a compass on the face of the depth," with the marginal note reading, 'or a circle.' But this source is perhaps too obvious. Says Mr. Fletcher:

Milton's commentators have almost wholly called attention to the reading of the Authorized Version as the source of Milton's usage, and have been content with having done so [infra!]. To accept this explanation of the word *compasses*, while quite justifiable so far as the basic idea of Milton's lines and of the Biblical passage is concerned, lays the poet open to the grave charge of having either misunderstood or mistranslated the Hebrew original in which the word is clearly חוג, *circle* .... As I have already stated no commentator is of much assistance in understanding what has happened here, and, as there is the possibility of charging Milton with a lack of knowledge with the Hebrew, the point becomes one which it is necessary for us to investigate.[31]

Assuredly, it does. The possibility of "lack of knowledge with the Hebrew" is a matter of philological interest, and at least Milton can be cleared of this grave charge. To begin with, there is no problem whatsoever in Milton's use of the word "compass." The Hebrew original does indeed mean a circle[32] as could clearly be deduced from the marginal note of the Authorized Version. But since neither the Authorized Version nor the common literary usage is adequate,

But even with Dante as an example it is extremely doubtful if he would have so far deviated from the Hebrew text as to have made the change from *circle* (חוג) to *compass* (מחוגה) had he not more direct and authoritative warrant for it than mere literary usage. Such direct and authoritative usage he found ready at hand in the commentaries of the rabbis on the Proverbs passage in the Buxtorf.[33]

Milton presumably had to consult the rabbis for the authoritative warrant to use "compasses." At any rate, the problem, by these terms, is narrowed to a linguistic one. Assuming for a moment, then, that the Authorized Version, the mere literary usage,[34] as well as the poetically preferable "compass" (as against "circle"), did not concern Milton so much as the philological implications of חוג, he could have found both suggestion and authority for the "compass" usage without recourse to the rabbis in the Buxtorf Bible. In the lexicons of the day there was sufficient authority, surely. The verb form of the word could have given him a clew. Both the lexicons of Schindler[35] and Leigh[36] show that it can mean "to draw around with a compass" (*circino circumscripsit*), and in Buxtorf's lexicon,[37] the standard Hebrew reference of the period, Milton would have noted the actual translation for the passage in Proverbs, *et cum circinavit circulum.* Even if for purposes of checking this apparently vital problem of translation Milton had neglected the elementary procedure of checking the verb form, he still could have found under the noun in Schindler[38] the explanation that the rabbis denote חוג as "compass." By modern standards this could perhaps be considered too free (although in Harkavy's *Students' Hebrew and Chaldee Dictionary to the Old Testament*, 1918, "compass" is given as one of the regular meanings of חוג), but Milton's references after all were seventeenth-century dictionaries. With respect to seventeenth-century English usage of "compass" and "circle," it may be added parenthetically, the words were sometimes interchangeable. Most of the exegetes of the period found the חוג problem unworthy of mention although Milton's countryman, Baynes, defines it: חוג *vel circinus est, quo describitur circulus* [and pointedly adds] *quamvis grammatico* מחוגה *circinum vocant.*[39] Whatever the reason Milton had for the usage, his understanding of the Hebrew can scarcely be challenged, much less his following the great translation of the Authorized Version.

The other example where Milton's literal translation of Scripture could serve as good authority for poetic usage is in his familiar figure of the Spirit of God impregnating chaos:

> Thou from the first
> Wast present, and with mighty wings outspread
> Dove-like satst brooding on the vast Abyss
> And mad'st it pregnant;[40]

and again:

> His brooding wings the Spirit of God outspread
> And vital vertue infus'd, and vital warmth
> Throughout the fluid mass.[41]

The antiquity and frequent occurrence of this conception have long been known by Milton scholars; Du Bartas, as well as the rabbis, has been singled out as a possible source within the enormous range of possibilities.[42] It is well known that "brooding" is a literal translation of מרחפת, and Milton's adherence to the Hebrew rather than the Authorized Version "moved" has been noted by Milton editors. Whatever nuances were suggested by other sources for his poetic usage, Scripture, it seems reasonable to assume, was most certainly the source for Milton's understanding of the creation process. Whatever his final decision as to the role of the Holy Spirit in creation,[43] in discussing Genesis 1:2, whether considering spirit as the Son[44] or as a manifestation of God's divine power,[45] the functional verb is rendered by Milton *incubabat*. Bishop Sumner in his English translation of the *De Doctrina* fails to translate Milton's original properly, substituting the Authorized Version's "moved" in every instance of Milton's *incubabat*. Of this rendition, which Milton would have found in most lexicons, and which was frequently mentioned by well-known commentators, Milton has to say (describing the Spirit as the divine breath by which all things are nourished): "*quomodo loco illum* Gen. 1:2 *spiritus Dei incubabat, multi intelligunt et antiqui et recentiores.*"[46] Which is at once an acknowledgment of his familiarity with exegetes *antiqui et recentiores* and evidence of his literal accuracy in the translation of Hebrew.

The significant point about both of these instances is that, granting some influence of the Bible on *Paradise Lost*, the figure in question in each case could be simply derived from the literal translation of Scripture. Suggested parallels with other sources, in these cases, do not seem particularly consequential.

Milton was not a specialist in Hebrew nor a student of the rabbinical literature; but it is evident that for the Hebrew text of the Bible he was, to use the words of Sandys —and with emphasis—a good general scholar.

IV

Rabbinical Exegesis

IT HAS BEEN SHOWN that the hermeneutic basis of the *De Doctrina*, Scripture alone under divine guidance, must, as defined by Milton, eliminate any dependence on the doctrinal deductions of theologians, be they patristic, contemporary, or rabbinical. Doctrines must proceed solely from Scripture. Milton's perusal of Scripture meant simply the discovery of the literal meaning of the Word of God, which resulted from diligent study of the text (for which grammatical authority could be sought), and, then, for the significance of the resultant rendition, dependence on the Holy Spirit. The claim of Harris Fletcher, therefore, that Milton depended so strongly, and in a few cases solely, upon rabbinical exegesis for his own formulation of various theological conceptions must, if true, completely contradict Milton's own delineation of his *modus operandi* of Biblical criticism. As matter for embellishment of poetic conception in *Paradise Lost*, extra-Biblical Hebraic material and rabbinical commentaries may be of some interest, but his supposed dependence on rabbinical commentary for some of the conclusions in the *De Doctrina* is another question.[1] Since Mr. Fletcher has attributed so finally to Milton's reading of the rabbis various conceptions of his theological system, Mr. Fletcher's hypothesis must either be correct and, accordingly, render Milton's hermeneutic professions very inexact, or else, in this instance, Mr.

Fletcher has erred and Milton's professions are consistent with practice in the *De Doctrina*.

There are two aspects to the problem of Milton's rabbinical readings. Firstly, there is the hermeneutical aspect of Milton's dependence upon any human authority (other than grammatical or lexicographic) for understanding Scripture, and secondly, there is the exegetical aspect as to his capacity or need to read rabbinical Hebrew at all. Related to these, of course, is the value of the whole corpus of rabbinical literature for Milton studies.

The case for the great influence of the rabbis rests upon direct evidence observed in Milton's prose and, to a lesser degree, upon indirect evidence inferred from *Paradise Lost*. The direct evidence, which is of chief importance (the indirect being of little moment without the substantiation of the direct), besides indicating, according to Mr. Fletcher, Milton's extensive use of Buxtorf's Rabbinical Bible, is used to substantiate the very important and necessary conclusion that Milton could and did read rabbinical Hebrew. From here it follows naturally that a truly enormous amount of new material for Milton study would at once be opened up.[2] It is necessary then, particularly in terms of the latter possibility, to determine whether or not the commentaries of Rashi, Ibn Ezra, Gersonides, and Kimchi[3] can be, in certain cases, the only possible exegetical source of Milton. When Mr. Fletcher concludes that no other source except the Buxtorf Bible will provide Milton with certain exegetical data, he establishes both contentions. While it has appeared in the previous chapter that there is little likelihood that Milton was familiar with anything more than the text of the Hebrew Bible, both this and the larger question of Milton's hermeneutics must be finally resolved in a test of Mr. Fletcher's direct proof.

In *An Apology against a Pamphlet against Smectymnuus*
occur the first references in Milton's prose to rabbinical
exegesis, and from them Mr. Fletcher has found indubita-
ble indication that Milton was reading the rabbinical commentary of the Buxtorf Rabbinical Bible. The passage in
the *Apology* has:

And this I shall easily averre though it may seeme a hard saying, that the Spirit of God who is purity it selfe, when he would
reprove any fault severely, or but relate things done or said with
indignation by others, abstains not from some words not civill
at other times to be spok'n. Omitting that place in Numbers at
the killing of *Zimri and Cosbi* done by Phineas in the heighth of
zeal, related as the Rabbines expound, not without an obscene
word, we may finde in Deuteronomy and three of the Prophets,
where God denouncing bitterly the punishments of Idolaters,
tels them in a terme immodest to be utter'd in coole blood, that
their wives shall be defil'd openly. But these, they will say were
honest words in that age when they were spok'n. Which is more
then any Rabbin can prove, and certainly had God been so
minded, he could have pickt such words, as should never have
come into abuse. What will they say to this. *David* going against
Nabal, in the very same breath when he had but just before
nam'd the *name of God*, he vowes not *to leave any alive of Nabal's
house that pisseth against the wall*. But this was unadvisedly
spoke, you will answer, and set downe to aggravate his infirmity.
Turne then to the first of Kings where God himselfe uses the
phrase; *I will cut off from Jereboam him that pisseth against the
wall*. Which had it beene an unseemely speech in the heat of an
earnest expression, then we must conclude that *Jonathan, or
Onkelos the Targumists* were of cleaner language then he that
made the tongue; for they render it as briefly, *I will cut off all
who are at yeares of discretion*, that is to say so much discretion
as to hide nakednesse. Whereas God who is the author both of
purity and eloquence, chose this phrase as fittest in that vehe-
ment character wherein he spake. Otherwise that plaine word
might have easily bin forborne. Which the *Masoreths* and Rab-
binicall *Scholiasts* not well attending, have often us'd to blurre

the margent with *Keri*, instead of *Ketiv*, and gave us this insuls rule out of their *Talmud*, *That all words which in the Law are writ obscenely, must be chang'd to more civill words*. Fools who would teach men to read more decently then God thought good to write.[4]

Milton here is arguing that he can justify the violence of his language (which in his more aggressive pamphlets is not noted for delicacy of expression) by appeal to Scripture. He has stated that in a passage in the Book of Numbers[5] the rabbinical explanation contains a more obscene word than the text itself. The reference, however, to what "the Rabbines expound" causes Mr. Fletcher to observe:

No translation of the Old Testament will aid us here. The English translations, including his favorite, the Authorized Version, in neither text nor in commentaries, provides an explanation of what Milton has said here. Nor will any text clarify his statement. If Latin commentaries are invoked, and Milton has elsewhere suggested a number of them, they yield nothing to the point here. But Milton did not say that some commentary had explained the passage "not without an obscene word." He specifically stated that he was speaking of "rabbis."[6]

That Milton specifically spoke of rabbis surely does not preclude any but a purely rabbinical source for his statement. It is true that no translation of the text will explain Milton's point,[7] but it is not at all evident that an explanation must rest upon any translation except Milton's own. The actual information that Milton used simply amounted to the fact that an explanation by the rabbis of a Hebrew word in Numbers contained an obscene word. But Mr. Fletcher explains that there is but one form of the text in which there is a possibility for obscenity, namely, the Hebrew original. In the Hebrew, it is observed that the phrase אל הקבה causes some difficulty:

The chief reason for this difficulty is that this verse contains two very similar expressions. The first of these אל הקבה clearly means "into the pavilion." The second phrase קבתה אל, is very similar to the first in spelling and appearance, and may have been connected with it in derivation. It denotes the precise part of the anatomy of Cosbi into which the spear was thrust.[8]

The question is then asked how Milton or any other Englishman of his day could have secured rabbinical commentaries to Scripture, which of course leads to the Buxtorf. Therefore:

Assuming for the moment that Milton had access to a Rabbinical Bible, the rabbis who commented on this verse in Numbers should determine whether he actually used their commentaries or not. His statement concerning their comment was of such a nature that, unless he read them, what he said of their comment would betray the fact. But if what he has said of them agrees with their comment, he must have read that comment.[9]

This preamble to the citation of the rabbinical commentary does not seem especially logical. In substance, we are told that if we find the obscene word in the rabbinical commentary, then Milton must have read the very comment. In other words, there was no other source for the simple information that the rabbinical gloss to the passage contained an obscene word except by the discovery of the actual rabbinical commentary. At this point Mr. Fletcher cites from the Buxtorf the commentaries of Rashi and Ibn Ezra which explain the phrase אל קבתה as the genitalia. Since Rashi specifically names the male and female genitalia, which is more obscene than the text itself, Mr. Fletcher sums up the whole matter by concluding:

To understand Milton's statement about the Numbers passage is, therefore, to realize that he was here using a Rabbinical Bible, and, what is more, to connect him with the commentaries of two rabbis, Rashi and Ibn Ezra...... Contact with the commentaries, as found in Buxtorf, of these two rabbis is now afforded him, his ability to read their peculiar jargon in its original being attested by his citation.[10]

This admittedly is an impressive proof, and Mr. Fletcher's arguments have been quoted fully in order that the basis for the rabbinical readings hypothesis be quite clear.

It is very probable, as suggested, that the phrase אל קבתה in the original did cause some difficulty. Milton, always an independent translator, confronted with such a problem of rendition, would naturally consult a Hebrew dictionary. Schindler's lexicon,[11] discussed in *Milton's Rabbinical Readings* as an available tool of Milton's period[12] and one that by the citation of Weemse (the only seventeenth-century lexicon that Weemse does mention incidentally) affords us, as Mr. Fletcher says, "the best possible evidence that such works were being used in England during the first quarter of the seventeenth century,"[13] proves to be exceedingly revealing on the problem. In the article under קבה, Schindler has not only the usual definition, but the very reference to the Numbers passage with an explanation of the phrases אל הקבה and אל קבתה. Most important, however, for our interest is Schindler's closing comment that the rabbis interpret the phrase as the (specifically named) female genitals. Thus Schindler:

Nom. קָבָה Chald. קָבָא Syr. קבות Arab. קבה Cubba tabernaculum, tentorium, papilio, cavea, aedicula, sacellum, testudo, aedificij, fornix, prostiliulum, lupanar. Num. 25 v.8 et ingressus est post virum Israelitem אֶל הַקֻבָּה, Targ. in tentorium: et transfodit ambos, virum Israelitem, et istam mulierem אֶל קֻבָתָה in tentorio ejus. pro קֻבָּתָה sine dages, Targ לִמְעָהָא ad viscera ejus. Accepit pro קֻבָה venter, saculus viscerum. LXX διὰ τῆς μήτρας αὐτῆς per vulvam ejus. *Rabbini intelligunt pudendum mulieris.*[14]

Milton's reference for the obscene word of the rabbis could easily—and most probably—have come from a lexicon. The actual problem of translation was not unknown to other commentators. Vatablus[15] in his notes to the Stephanus Bible qualifies his translation, *in locis genitalibus* by the specific note *mulieris sive in pudendis ejus*,[16] and Poole[17] cites Drusius and others for the same rendition.

Actually, the passage from the *Apology* affords us a rather interesting and typical expression of Milton's hermeneutics. His scorn for the rabbinical tampering with God's choice of words ("God, who is the author both of purity and eloquence") strongly recalls Chillingworth's attitude toward the interpretations of theologians who substituted their phrases for the plain words of Scripture. The whole criticism of the rabbinical phrasing demonstrates Milton's rigorous adherence to the pure text of Scripture, and the "insulse rule" out of the Talmud stands as the antithesis of Milton's approach to the Bible.

In this same passage there is another statement that contains evidence that is, in Mr. Fletcher's opinion, "equally enlightening in connection with his use of rabbinical material and shows even more clearly than the portion just examined [the obscene word of Numbers 25:8] that he was using a rabbinical Bible and rabbinical commentaries."[18] The reference in this case is to Milton's remark that there is a verse in Deuteronomy [28:30] which contains an expression too indecent to be uttered in cold blood and which, he added, occurs also in three of the Prophets. His whole discussion at this point becomes meaningless, according to Fletcher, unless it is clearly understood that Milton was basing his argument on the Deuteronomy passage from his study of the Qere and Khetiv[19] of the Rabbinical Bible, the only form of the Hebrew text that could provide such commentary.

It is supposed that Milton's attention to the rabbinical commentaries was a result of his having noticed that the *Qere* for the word ישגלנה , "to violate," was ישכבנה "to lie with," a refinement of meaning, to be sure.

To explain what Mr. Fletcher calls the complicated arguments contained in Milton's allusion, it is pointed out that only through the Hebrew, שגל , can the passage in the Prophets which contains the same word be located at all, an observation that certainly seems reasonably apparent. The rabbinical notes to the Deuteronomy passage and to the passages in the three other prophets (Isaiah 13:15, Zechariah 14:2, and Jeremiah 3:2) are cited which show Milton's remark to be accurate, and further, that,

Milton's statement is evidence that he had read not only the קרי of the margin for the textual כתיב for any person able to read Hebrew could at least point this out; but also what for us is much more important, the rabbinical commentaries to the passage.[20]

As in the Numbers passage, Milton's statement is not evidence that has any necessary bearing on the use of rabbinical commentaries. The existence of rabbinical Qere and Khetiv was known to any serious student of the Bible, and explanations of textual variants with copious illustration of their occurrence in Scripture were normally available in the Hebrew lexicons of the period. For instance, mention of the "margents" on the Deuteronomy passage in question is made in a general discussion of Qere and Khetiv by Weemse who remarks of the Massoretes: "They will not say *Subagitabit Eam, He shall know her* as the Text hath it; but in the margent, He shall lye with her."[21]

More consequential however is the lexicographic data. Buxtorf's *Lexicon Chaldaicum Talmudicum et Rabbinicum* defines שגל "to ravish" (the root of ישגלנה of Deuteronomy 28:30) *vitiare violare virginem aut mulierem. Verbum fuit olim in comuni sermone obscoenum, unde ubi in sacro textu Hebraeo occurrit, ibi pro eo legitur verbum* שָׁכַב ["to sleep with," or "to lie with"].[22] So far as the mention of the three other Prophets, there are references to the occurrence of the softening of שגל in these passages in the lexicons of both Schindler and Buxtorf. It is clear that the proof of Milton's rabbinical readings must be sought elsewhere.

In the remainder of what seems to be Milton's most significant allusions to the rabbis, that part of the *Apology* passage where Milton is discussing the nature of an instance in Scripture which contains a threat by David[23] and another threat in the same words by God himself,[24] a reference to the Targum is made.[25]

Mention of the Targum completes finally for Mr. Fletcher the evidence for Milton's use of the Rabbinical Bible:

Both of the passages to which Milton has referred are softened in the Targum. He referred in the second instance to the change from the Hebrew *mingentem ad parietem* to the Aramaic 'who are at years of discretion,' and this change actually occurs in the two texts mentioned, the Hebrew reading משתין בקיר and the Aramaic ידע   מדע in the Targum. Now the importance of this statement by Milton is not so much in its clear indication of his ability to use the Targums, for his knowledge of them is well authenticated on other grounds. But, his citation of a Targum reading in connection with the other elements he has cited, the Hebrew text, the marginal *qere*, and rabbinical commentaries, all these taken together make certain the form of Biblical text he was here using. There is no other Biblical text except the rabbinical, which assembles all of these elements at one time.[26]

Turing to the handy lexicon, we find that Schindler has under שתן a translation of the Targum reading for Samuel 25:22 and an explanation of the word's connotation in the text of the Bible. Thus Schindler:

שתן Inde Benoni Hiphil מַשְׁתִּין mingens I Sam.25 v.22 Si reliquero מַשְׁתִּין *Mingentem ad parietem*, Significat aetatem puerilem, quam non pudet mingere ad parietem. Nihil relinguam. Targ. יָדַע מַדָע *scientem scientiam*: filium intelligentem.[27]

Further information, as well as a refreshingly informal exegesis concerning the Targum to Samuel 25:22, was available to Milton in the English of Weemse's *Christian Synagogue*. Weemse also translates the Targum reading:

He shall not leave one to pisse against the wall mingentem ad parietem: that is, *He shall not leave a young man*: for such was the modestie of the men when they came of age, that they went aside where they might not bee seene; but the little children which were not ashamed stood up against the wall. It is not meant of a dogge here, Targum translates it, *filium intelligentum a childe of understanding.* [Milton's "years of discretion."][28]

So much for the Targum; but before leaving the *Apology* passage, it is necessary to discuss one last point. Because of Milton's example of שגל from the previously discussed passage of Deuteronomy (28:30), his mention of the "insulse rule" out of the Talmud in connection with it (speaking, of course, of the *Apology* passage as a whole), there is still one more part of what Mr. Fletcher describes as the chain of evidence for Milton's use of the Buxtorf Rabbinical Bible. Although allowing that Milton probably did not take the rule out of the Talmud itself, Mr.

Fletcher continues: "Milton would have found it stated twice in the Introduction to Buxtorf's *Rabbinical Bible*, using the same word in the same passages from Deuteronomy and the Prophets as he cited in the passage we have quoted above."[29]

There follows a quotation from Buxtorf's Introduction (a revision of the Introduction written by Rabbi Jacob ben Chajim ibn Adonijah for the Bomberg Rabbinical Bible)[30] which contains the rule quoted by Milton and the specific example of שגל in the passages mentioned. The evidence is accordingly summarized:

It is important, it seems to me, to notice Milton's citation of this Talmudic rule, using the same forms found in the Introduction by Jacob in Buxtorf's Bible, because this fact adds its evidence to Milton's having used that work. The use of שגל as an example of the rule both by Milton and Jacob leads inevitably to the conclusion that Milton took the rule from this source rather than another."[31]

There were other sources available to Milton for the Talmud rule besides the Buxtorf Rabbinical Bible. Most pertinent to the argument of inevitability suggested above is the citation and discussion of the rule in Hottinger's well-known *Thesaurus Philologicus*. Hottinger uses the example of שגל, refers to the passages of Deuteronomy, Isaiah, and Zechariah, and specifically quotes the reason for the whole procedure that Milton so sarcastically attacked:

Alios verecundiae causa mutatas, ut cum voces, quae flexu temporis obscoenae esse coeperunt, verecundioribus exprimuntur, juxta Canonem . . . . *Omnes voces, quae* scriptae *sunt in lege* (hoc est verbo Dei) inhoneste, (id est, minus verecundae pronunciatu) *legunt, seu legendum tradiderunt eas honeste* . . . . De voce שָׁגֵל pro qua nunc legunt שכב Deut.28 v.30 Jesa.13 v.16 Zach.14. v.2 . . . . Cum vero paulatim obscoenus esse coepisset ejus usus actumque venereum denotaret, Doctores Judaei illi verecundius suffecerunt verbum שכב. Est enim lingua Hebraea, et hoc etiam nomine vocata sancta, quod decore, sancte, modeste, omnia exprimeret.[32]

There remain of Mr. Fletcher's direct evidence of Milton's rabbinical readings two passages from Milton's prose, one linguistic and the other a citation of specific rabbis. The first occurs in *Of Prelatical Episcopacy* where Milton makes the statement "let him feare lest he and his Baal be turned into Bosheth."[33] While it is pointed out that modern lexicons explain the phrase as a scribal peculiarity which occurs in the Hebrew text,[34] Mr. Fletcher insists:

But in Milton's day, no lexicon explained this, though for his usage in the passage quoted, he would not have needed a lexicon to have understood the substitution and what it meant. The rabbinical commentaries to the passages in Scripture where the change has been made would have been sufficient. From this comment alone, Milton would have been supplied with ample explanation of what the changing of *Baal* into *Bosheth* meant and represented.[35]

Doubtless the marginalia of the Buxtorf would have sufficed, but a lexicon (despite this assurance of their uselessness in the matter) would have been a readier source. Turning then to Schindler's Lexicon, it is not surprising to find under בעל (baal) the explanation that it is the same as בשת (bosheth), with a further reference to see the word בוש, under which it is stated that בשת is בעל by metonomy. Schindler has:

[For בעל] Et quia בעל baal, et boschet idem sunt, idolum videlicet: ideo vocatur et ירבשת Ierubbeseth. 2 Sam. ii v. 21 de quo in בוש vide[36] [Under בוש] Deinde בשת Pudor, per metonymiam, est בעל idolum cujus pudet cultorem, postquam ab eo in periculis destitutus, nec adjutus fuerit.[37]

Grotius explains the metonomy of בשת for בעל [idolum] in his exegesis on Jeremiah 3:24,[38] and a full explanation of the phrase was also available in Bochart, Glass, and Piscator.[39]

The last passage to be examined is in the *Doctrine and Discipline of Divorce*. Milton, with no little forensic effort, cites Judges 19:2 as further evidence that divorce should be granted for causes other than adultery:

He [Grotius] shews also that fornication is tak'n in Scripture for such a continual headstrong behaviour, as tends to plain contempt of the husband: and proves it out of Judges 19:2, where the Levites wife is said to have plaid the whoore against him; which Josephus and the Septuagint, with the Chaldean, interpret onely of stubbornesse and rebellion against her husband: and to this I adde that Kimchi and the two other Rabbies who glosse the text, are in the same opinion. Ben Gerson reasons, that had it bin whooredome, a Jew and a Levite would have disdain'd to fetch her again. And this I shall contribute, that had it beene whoordome, she would have chosen any other place to run to, then to her father's house, it being so infamous for an Hebrew woman to play the harlot, and so opprobrious to the parents.[40]

This passage contains the only reference to a specific rabbinical gloss in all Milton's writings. The mention of Kimchi and Gersonides, coupled with the paraphrase of Gersonides's commentary, plainly show that Milton was referring to the rabbinical commentary on Judges. This is no proof, however, that he consulted that commentary in the original, nor, far less, does it indicate extensive readings of the rabbis. It is merely evidence that he used the reference to embellish an argument. In light of the quantity of material dealing with rabbinical commentary that was available to Milton there is nothing unusual about his acquaintance with the distinguished names of Gersonides and Kimchi. Certainly, it is not likely that Milton learned rabbinical Hebrew solely for the purpose of adding two sentences to his divorce tract, particularly when those sentences merely substantiate an already thoroughly proved point. The citation of Grotius, the Septuagint,[41] Josephus, and the Targum ("The Chaldean") was adequate authority for a position that was in his day known to anyone who consulted Biblical commentaries. A gloss of the passage containing the same explanation of the text as Milton's occurs as early as Wyclif. That the translation of זנה in the Authorized Version as "playing the whore" should have been translated in a less literal sense was well known to exegetes, and Drusius cites Rashi and Kimchi on the point.[42] For the specific purpose of additional argument for a not very popular point of view on divorce, his attention having been drawn to the rabbinical gloss on Judges 19:2 from the references of other exegetes, he may well have secured direct assistance in checking the rabbinical commentary.

There remains, of course, the possibility that Milton consulted a paraphrase or even a translation of the commentaries. That at least one such translation existed is established by Imbonatus who mentions the detailed contents of a literal translation of the commentaries by Conradus Pellicanus and specifically notes that the complete commentaries of Gersonides, Kimchi, and Ibn Ezra for the Book of Judges were translated into Latin.[43]

The question of Milton's use of the rabbis for his conceptions of the creation will be noticed in the discussion of his materialism; but in light of the material suggested in this chapter, it seems reasonable to assume that the case for the necessity of Milton's use of rabbinical commentaries is disproved. From what has been remarked earlier of his hermeneutics, the likelihood of his dependence on the Buxtorf commentaries seems wholly improbable; and since there is no evidence to show that he could or did read rabbinic Hebrew (rather, as we have seen, what evidence we possess indicates clearly a knowledge of pointed Biblical Hebrew), the usefulness or relevance of the whole corpus of medieval rabbinic exegesis to Milton studies must be considered very doubtful indeed.

Milton on Bara: the Creation

OF ALL MILTON'S HETERODOXIES the least discussed, and the most significant from the standpoint of his theory and practice of Biblical criticism, is his so-called "materialism." Like pantheism it is, though technically justifiable, a misleading term because the natural tendency is to link Milton with the philosophic school under that category. Under such an impression sources for Milton's idea could be attributed, as has actually been the case, to specific materialists and pantheists.[1] But the gross resemblances inevitably present between their materialism or pantheism and Milton's *ex Deo* conception of the cosmos serve as no indication of Milton's derivation of a strictly theological tenet. For Milton's position, despite the similarities of Plato, Lucretius, Philo, Eriugena, Servetus, Gerson, Ibn Ezra, Fludd, Boehme, and others, is uniquely his and was independently derived from his exegetical conclusions alone.[2] No precise parallel can, in fact, be found between Milton's conception of the creation and that of any other.[3] To examine the hexaemeral literature is of no avail here for the simple reason that Milton did not believe in the orthodox creation *ex nihilo* but a creation from a pre-existent matter which proceeded somewhere in time out of God Himself.

The inevitable starting point for Milton—and for our analysis—is the meaning of the original text of Scripture. As against those who uphold the *ex nihilo* position, Mil-

ton's exegesis of the opening phrase of Genesis (בְּרָא אלהים
בראשית) defines the all-important verb ברא (*create*) as
signifying on the contrary creation out of matter:

Most of the moderns contend that it was formed from nothing,
a basis as unsubstantial as that of their own theory. In the first
place, it is certain that neither the Hebrew verb ברא, nor the
Greek χτίζειν, nor the Latin *creare*, can signify to create out of
nothing. On the contrary, these words uniformly signify to
create out of matter.[4]

Here is no problem of philosophic speculation nor related
exegetical commentary. For Milton the origin of doctrine
must begin with Scripture. He did not first formulate
doctrine and then seek to support it from Scripture. Milton was not straining to labor a remote interpretation of
ברא in order to prove a preconceived theory of creation.
On the contrary, the position is completely established by
the literal meaning, the unquestionable translation, of the
actual word in the Scriptures. Milton's ברא by definition
cannot mean creation out of nothing.

Whatever difficulties follow as a necessary consequence
of the meaning of Scripture must be in some way resolved,
but there can be no alternative. Milton argues simply that
according to the text it is certain that the world was
created out of matter of some kind (*ex materia igitur
quacumque mundum fuisse conditum palam est*).[5]

What authority had Milton for the linguistic assertion
that irrevocably formed the basis of his entire conception
of the creation? The answer to this, it is clear, must concern philological rather than theological sources. The
problem is one of translation, not conception. Patently,
the grammarians must be the sole arbiters of the point,
and it should be of some importance if it is found that
Milton's translation of ברא was a generally known and

established philological datum. Most of the lexicons, merely by noting the various occurrences of ברא in other parts of Scripture where it is obvious that the verb does not mean to create out of nothing, show without stating the fact that strictly the *ex nihilo* qualification is theological rather than grammatical. In the nonscriptural lexicons the *ex nihilo* sense of the verb "to create" was ignored. The *Dictionarium Octolinguarum* of Calepinus, for example, only notes a Ciceronian usage of "create" and defines the words (*creo*, χτίζειν, and ברא) as simply *producere*.[6] Leigh, however, goes into considerable detail in his *Critica Sacra* under ברא to show that it can mean to create *ex praejente materia*. He notes the Septuagint use of ποιέω for ברא , lists the Greek and Latin sense of "produce from something," and quotes Fagius on the duplicate meaning of ברא, "*usurpari etiam hoc verbum ubi aliquid non ex mero nihilo, sed ex praejacente materia fit.*"[7]

Far from being a slighted point in the commentaries, we find the linguistic fact of the literal translation of ברא used by Milton (generally noted but never followed) in the exegesis of Pareus, Rivetus, Zanchius, Episcopius, and Fagius, to name only those theologians mentioned in his other works. Rivetus in his discussion actually includes (as did Milton) the Greek and the Latin: "Si tamen vocem spectemus per se, neque verbum ברא bara, Ebraeum, neque verbum χτίζειν Graecum, neque *creare* Latinum, ad propriam illam significationem *producendi ex nihilo aliquid*, restringi potest."[8]

Episcopius also mentions ברא and alludes to the occurrence of the word in other passages:

Fateor quidem eos frustra esse, qui ex verbo ברא sententiam istam [i.e., the *ex nihilo* position] adstruere laborant. Certum enim est verbum istud, uti et Graecum χτίζειν, vix unquam, saltem non nisi rarissime significare productionem rei ex nihilo, nedum ut ex vi sua et per se eam significet; frequentissime vero, vel novi atque eximi alicujus operis patrationem vel accedentium mirabilium effectionem, vel refectionem et restaurationem rerum, qui Hebraei compositis verbis carent: Prout patet ex locis variis, quae hic compilare ex aliis scriptoribus non est necesse.[9]

Pareus merely notes that *verbum quidem creare Latina usurpatione proprie non est ex nihilo aliquid efficere* but like Zanchius reviews at great length the arguments pro and con for the *ex nihilo* conception.[10] Needless to say, none of these theologians who mentioned the *literal* sense of ברא believed in anything but the orthodox view.[11]

Certainly the philological position of Milton was widely acknowledged. The orthodox commentators ("Moderni"), who admitted the precise translation of ברא did not mean *ex nihilo creare* but upheld, nevertheless, the *ex nihilo* tenet, were of no consequence to Milton. All that was of any significance to the framer of the *De Doctrina* was the proper and true meaning of the word in Scripture. To those theologians who followed the orthodox view despite what was to him the plain evidence of Scripture, Milton scornfully remarks:

To allege, therefore, that creation signifies production out of nothing, is, as logicians say, to lay down premises without a proof; for the passages of Scripture commonly quoted for this purpose, are so far from confirming the received opinion, that they rather imply the contrary; namely, that all things were not made out of nothing.[12]

Having determined the true meaning of the passage and since *et Scriptura Sacra et rationi ipsa suggerat*, Milton proceeds to consider the doctrinal consequences of his exegesis.

For since action and passion are relative terms, and since, consequently, no agent can act externally, unless there be some patient, such as matter, it appears impossible that God could have created this world out of nothing; not from any defect of power on his part, but because it was necessary that something should have previously existed capable of receiving passively the exertion of the divine efficacy. Since, therefore, both Scripture and reason concur in pronouncing that all these things were made, not out of nothing, but out of matter, it necessarily follows, that matter must either have always existed independently of God, or have originated from God at some particular point of time. That matter should have been always independent of God, seeing that it is only a passive principle, dependent on the Deity, and subservient to him; and seeing, moreover, that, as in number, considered abstractedly, so also in time or eternity there is no inherent force or efficacy; that matter, I say, should have existed of itself from all eternity, is inconceivable. If on the contrary it did not exist from all eternity, it is difficult to understand from whence it derives its origin. There remains, therefore, but one solution of the difficulty, for which moreover we have the authority of Scripture, namely, that all things are of God.[13]

The only solution for which there is the authority of Scripture, that all things are out of God, must follow, since matter could not have been independent of God if it existed from the beginning nor could it have existed by itself as a passive principle dependent on Deity. At this point, Milton was not unaware that his adherence to the literal text was leading him into uncomfortable speculations; and somewhat defensively he goes into the question of God's corporeal nature and concludes with some labor that matter was not originally imperfect in its own nature but proceeded like the angels incorruptible from God and even since the Fall remains incorruptible in essence.[14] However the climax of Milton's doctrinal aberrations from orthodoxy is reached when he finds it necessary to limit the power of God:

Since therefore it has (as I conceive) been satisfactorily proved, under the guidance of Scripture, that God did not produce everything out of nothing, but of himself, I proceed to consider the necessary consequence of this doctrine, namely, that if all things are not only from God, but of God, no created thing can be finally annihilated. And, not to mention that not a word is said of this annihilation in the sacred writings, there are other reasons, besides that which has been just alleged, and which is the strongest of all, why this doctrine should be altogether exploded. First, because God is neither willing, nor, properly speaking, able to annihilate anything altogether.[15]

Having proved through Scripture that God produced everything out of himself, Milton finds the necessary consequence of his doctrine to be that no created thing can be finally annihilated. God is neither willing nor able to annihilate anything altogether. This is proved in the fashion of an exercise in logic, and abruptly dropped as though Milton already was anticipating the difficulties he had made for himself in terms of death eternal and the final conflagration. Uncertain as he was on this latter question,[16] it appears, from his treatment of matter in *Paradise Lost*,[17] that he never discarded the idea of what Mr. Lovejoy has called the Great Chain of Being. Raphael's famous description seems clear:

> O Adam, one Almightie is, from whom
> All things proceed, and up to him return,
> If not depraved from good, created all
> Such to perfection, one first matter all,
> Indu'd with various forms, various degrees
> Of substance, and in things that live, of life.[18]

Although the conception was not developed nor even elaborated upon, there is evidence that the Socinians, like Milton, believed in creation from pre-existent matter

rather than the *ex nihilo*. Fock, indeed, who feels this to
be a corollary of the Socinian conception of the finite
world's thoroughly external relation to God,[19] maintains:
"Es kann nämlich kaum einen Zweifel unterworfen sein,
dass der Socinianismus keine Schöpfung aus Nichts,
sondern vielmehr eine Schöpfung aus einer präexistenten
Materie lehrt."[20]

Völkel,[21] in his *De Vera Religione* (a treatise described
as the most complete and best systematic treatment of
Socinianism),[22] appears to be fairly close to Milton, judging from his exegesis on two contradictory accounts of
creation which occur in the Apocrypha. According to
Völkel, the world was created out of nothing only in so
far as it was created out of formless matter:

Primo igitur de materia dicendum est, de qua contrariae in
speciem sententiam, sed revera eadem, in duobus apocryphis ut
vocant libris exstant. Nam lib.2 Machab. cap.7, 28 legimus,
Deum coelum et terram et omnia, quae in eis sunt, hominumque
ex nihilo fecisse. Auctor tamen libri sapientiae cap.11, 18 asserit,
Deum ex *informi materia* omnia creasse. Posterior locus prioris
est explicatio. Ideo enim Deus ex nihilo omnia fecisse dicitur,
quia ea creavit ex materia informi, hoc est ejusmodi, quae nec
actu nec naturali aliqua potentia seu inclinatione id fuerit, quod
postea ex ea fuit formatum, ita ut nisi vis quaedam infinita
accessisset, numquam quicquam ex ea fuisset exstiturum.[23]

This passage in 2 Maccabees, which has the world and
man created from nothing, according to Völkel, is to be
interpreted by the passage in the Book of Wisdom which
describes a creation from formless matter.

Creation, then, is God's bringing form out of the formless, which is quite like God's relation to Chaos in *Paradise
Lost*. But this general parallel, like those advanced by
others, is merely of interest as an observation; for Milton's
disavowal of the creation *ex nihilo*, unlike Völkel's metaphysical qualification of the two passages of the Apocry-

pha, derived entirely from his interpretation of Genesis 1:1. His position was determined (*Scriptura Duce*), not by philosophic deduction, but by the simple linguistic fact that the key verb of the text, despite the general theological interpretation to the contrary, did not *per se* mean "to create out of nothing." From this starting point he necessarily ("*quod necessario sequitur*") evolved his unique system of the material cosmos, the corollary of his exegesis.

Whatever the theological inconsistencies that resulted, Milton's deductions were logical in nature, and his speculations, far from being mystic or metaphysical, were typical of a rational Puritan interpretation of the plain sense of Scripture. Milton, keenly aware of his radical position throughout the development of his creation doctrine, followed with courage and consistency his hermeneutic declaration of independence:

Every believer has a right to interpret the Scriptures for himself, inasmuch as he has the Spirit for his guide, and the mind of Christ is in him; nay, the expositions of the public interpreter can be of no use to him, except so far as they are confirmed by his own conscience.[24]

Since he felt that the literal sense of ברא prevented any inference of *ex nihilo* as not following plainly from the meaning of the word, even more fully did he demonstrate his basic rule of exegesis, never to make any inferences from the sacred text except such as follow necessarily from the words themselves, lest what is not written is understood in place of what is written, "the shadow for the substance, the fallacies of human reasoning for the doctrines of God."[25]

For, he concludes, it is by the declarations of Scripture that our consciences are bound;[26] and so bound too, it might be added, was the theology of the *De Doctrina*.

Milton on Nephesh: the Soul

MILTON'S MORTALISM,[1] his belief that the soul dies with the body, though not so singular as his conception of creation, was, in his day, an exceedingly esoteric position.[2] Earlier, to be sure, there were attacks by Calvin and Lutz[3] on the related doctrine of psychopannychism (a subject of considerable controversy in the eighteenth century), and Pomponazzi's[4] views achieved some notoriety; but in the seventeenth century, aside from a few pamphlets[5] and the attribution of the belief to Anabaptists and Socinians, it was of no moment in the theological disputations of the age.

Nevertheless, we should expect here, as in the case of the creation, that Milton's espousal of a doctrine condemned by contemporary theologians must result directly from his independent exegesis; and, if our surmise is correct, the starting point should likewise be neither theological nor philosophical but simply a point of rendition of Scripture. From a translation of Scripture, the precise literal meaning, as rendered by Milton, the necessary doctrine would be resolved. Such a point of origin is clearly indicated by Milton's understanding of נֶפֶשׁ (soul), and, indeed, his entire formulation of the mortalist doctrine rests wholly upon this premise.

His point is fairly simple, namely that "soul" in the Old Testament refers to the whole man and that, therefore, the whole man is soul and the soul man. Beginning

his account of the visible creation, Milton says of Genesis
1:26 (God said, Let us make man in our own image, after
our own likeness) that it was not the body alone that was
then made but the soul of man also. This, he continues,
precludes the notion of the pre-existence of the soul (*quod
quidam somniant*); that notion is plainly refuted by Genesis 2:7 (God formed man of the dust of the ground, and he
breathed into his nostrils the breath of life; thus man became a living soul). Other passages are cited to show that
God also infused the breath of life into other beings; and
Milton sums up with the etymological observation that
the word "spirit" has no other meaning in Scripture but
that breath of life which we aspire, or the vital sensitive or
rational faculty, or some action or affection belonging to
that faculty.[6] At this point the main argument is presented:

Man having been created after this manner, it is said, as a consequence, that "man became a living soul"; whence it may be
inferred (unless we had rather take the heathen writers for our
teachers respecting the nature of the soul) that man is a living
being, intrinsically and properly one and individual, not compound or separable, not, according to the common opinion,
made up and framed of two distinct and different natures, as of
soul and body, but that the whole man is soul, and the soul man,
that is to say, a body, or substance individual, animated, sensitive, and rational; and that the breath of life was neither a part
of the divine essence, nor the soul itself, but as it were an inspiration of some divine virtue fitted for the exercise of life and
reason, and infused into the organic body; for man himself, the
whole man, when finally created, is called in express terms "a
living soul" . . . . Where however we speak of the body as of a
mere senseless stock, there the soul must be understood as signifying either the spirit, or its secondary faculties, the vital or
sensitive faculty for instance. Thus it is as often distinguished
from the spirit, as from the body itself. Luke i. 46, 47. I Thess.
v.23. "your whole spirit and soul and body." Heb. iv. 12. "to

the dividing asunder of soul and spirit." But that the spirit of
man should be separate from the body, so as to have a perfect
and intelligent existence independently of it, is nowhere said in
Scripture, and the doctrine is evidently at variance both with
nature and reason, as will be shown more fully hereafter. For the
word "soul" is also applied to every kind of living being; Gen.
i. 30. "to every beast of the earth," &c. "wherein there is life."
vii. 22. "all in whose nostrils was the breath of life, of all that
was in the dry land, died"; yet it is never inferred from these
expressions that the soul exists separate from the body in any
of the brute creation.[7]

There are two main theses here: First, exegetically, the
word "soul" means the organic whole of man and, indeed,
is used in Scripture for animal and every kind of living
being; second, hermeneutically, there is nothing said in
Scripture to indicate a separation of soul and body. This
has the Miltonic ring.

The critical phrase in Genesis 2:7 is לנפש חיה *anima
vivens*; and, before examining the speculations of Milton's
contemporaries on the question, it is necessary to check
with the lexicons, for these would be the first tool of reference in Milton's private perusal of Scripture.

Schindler gives several meanings for נפש, amply justi-
fying Milton's translation:

Plura autem vocabulo נפש animae significantur: 1. *halitus oris,
anhelitus spiritus* .... 2. *vita*, quae in motu et sensu consistit.
3. *anima rationalis* (Gen. 2:7) .... factus est homo .... in
animam vivam. Targum .... in spirituum loquentem, id est
rationalem .... 4. *corpus animatum, animal brutum* .... 5.
Homo .... 6. *Corpus* .... 7. *Persona*[8]

Buxtorf, too, gives as the first meanings *anima, vita,
corpus, animal,* and notes the use of *anima* for "*homine
corpore.*"[9]

More elaborate than either Schindler or Buxtorf, however, are the remarks of Milton's contemporary, Leigh. נפש he begins, is *anima*, but continues (like Schindler):

Plura autem hoc vocabulo significantur, 1. Halitus oris, anhelitus, spiritus, flatus, ventus Gen.1.20. *sic Animae nomen Latinis et Graecis pro Anhelitu sumitur*, pulmo animae praelargus anhelat. 2. Vita, *cujus anima fons est et origo*, Job 216. Psal.712,3. Prov.12.10 Psal.54.5. 3. Anima rationalis, quae est altera et principalior pars hominis, Gen.35.18. 4. Corpus animatum, animal brutum Gen.1.24.[10]

Following the same order as Schindler (which Leigh very probably consulted), *homo*, *cadaver*, and *appetitus* are recorded for the remaining meanings, which surely covers Milton's ground. In the margin even more is explained, and references to the controversial material on the subject are noted. In Leigh's marginalia, moreover, is the exact argument of Milton:

This Hebrew word Nephesh and the Greek ψυχή hath the name of breathing or respiring. The Latine *anima quasi anemos, id est, ventus*. The Chaldee is like the Hebrew, Naphsha. Observavi in omni lingua quae mihi aliquatenus nota esset, id est Graeca, Latina, Hebraea, Chaldaea, nomen animae eandem habere etymologiam . . . . Vox ebraea Nephesh praeter propriam notionem tropicas habet tres quarum singulae hic applicari possunt: 1. Enim per Synecdochen ipsam personam significat, Psal.11.1 anima hominis passim pro homine . . . . 2. Per Metonymiam effic. significat vitam . . . . 3. Per Metonymiam adjuncti, vel ut alii loquuntur, contenti, pro corpore . . . . Iunius in Psal.16.10 sic interpretatur.[11]

These remarks of Leigh explaining the basic etymology and the use of "soul" for "man," "life," or "body" (with the citation of Junius) were sufficient authority for the literalist position of Milton. But besides these standard lexicons, in Gataker's dissertation on the Hebraisms of the New Testament, a book widely known in the period and very likely consulted by Milton, is the very point of the "whole man" made in the *De Doctrina*. In the tenth chapter of his *De Novi Stylo* (which deals with the subject נפש *anima pro homine*), Gataker makes the following observations on the point of this synecdoche common to both Greek and Hebrew:

ψυχὴν animam pro homine usurpari; LXX Gen. c46 v27 . . . . At unde, inqis, Hebraismi illis innotuerunt, qibus nihil unqam fuit cum gente illâ commune? norunt omnes συνεκδοχικῶς partem pro integri usurpari. Estque hoc in genere linguae nullius non commune . . . . corpora ergò pro hominibus, servi maximè, Graecum est. Animae pro eisdem idiotismi Hebraici . . . . Hebraeorum illud peculiare non immerito censetur, qod animam, non pro vita tantum, vel etiam homine viventi, sive vità praedito; sed etiam pro homine mortuo et exanimi usurpant . . . . Certe Hebraeis sicut נפש, ψυχὴ anima pars altera [i.e. corpus] frequenter; ita בשר, σάρξ caro non minus familiariter . . . . sermo instituitur toto homine sive toto hominis.[12]

The philological authority for Milton's argument is unquestionable.[13] He also could have found most of his arguments cited but rebutted in the comments of Pareus and Rivetus on the theological implications of Genesis 2:7, but for Milton the transition from this philologically established meaning of Scripture to mortalism was more a corollary than a deduction. The Holy Scriptures, not theologians, determine doctrine.

Because the definition of death of the body is the loss of life, *privatio vitae sive extinctio*, and since the common definition that death consists in the separation of soul and body is inadmissible,[14] Milton concludes that, "Separatio igitur illa non est mors hominis dicenda."[15] As for theological opinion to the contrary:

Here then arises an important question, which, owing to the prejudice of divines in behalf of their preconceived opinions, has

usually been dismissed without examination, instead of being
treated with the attention it deserves. Is it the whole man, or
the body alone, that is deprived of vitality? And as this is a
subject which may be discussed without endangering our faith
or devotion, whichever side of the controversy we espouse, I
shall declare freely what seems to me the true doctrine, as collected from numberless passages of Scripture; without regarding
the opinion of those, who think that truth is to be sought in the
school of philosophy, rather than in the sacred writings.[16]

Though thus bound by the meaning and scriptural
usage of נפש to see in death the dissolution of the whole
man, body and soul, Milton approaches the exposition of
the doctrine with some consciousness of its radical nature,
just as he did in the creation doctrine. It is a subject, he
insists, that can be discussed without endangering faith
or devotion no matter which side of the controversy is
taken. So typically, in the face of the established theological position (which he refers to as arising out of prejudice
and preconceived opinions),[17] Milton is going to declare
freely—as collected from numberless passages of Scripture
—what seems to him the true doctrine, without regarding
the opinion of those who think that truth is to be found
in the schools of philosophy rather than in Scripture.

The argument itself is simply stated: "Inasmuch then
as the whole man is uniformly said to consist of body,
spirit, and soul . . . . I shall first show that the whole man
dies, and, secondly, that each component part suffers
privation of life."[18] God created the whole man, the whole
man dies.[19] What remains of the proof is, for Milton, the
strongest of all arguments. Commenting on I Corinthians
15:42–50, Milton points out that Paul's reasoning proceeds
on the supposition that there are only two states, the
mortal and the immortal, death and resurrection, and
nothing is said of any intermediate condition (*de statu*

autem ullo intermedio, ne verbum quidem).[20] Where Scripture is silent, man must not speculate. This is Milton's essential case for mortalism, necessarily dependent on the true meaning of נפש and the silence of Scripture on any intermediate state. The *whole man* conception of Genesis 2:7 is the rational foundation for the tenet.

What follows, the evidence of the numberless passages of Scripture, is more polemic than expository. Milton examines various passages of Scripture used to uphold the opposite doctrine and, in disproving them, sometimes descends to mere cavil. Some passages he refutes linguistically either by appeal to a separate text[21] or recourse to Biblical idiom,[22] but most of them are labored. Two of them, however, are extremely interesting because of the similar exegesis of Socinians. The first is concerned with punctuation of the text. Milton says of Luke 23:43 (*Jesus said unto him, verily I say unto thee, Today shalt thou be with me in paradise*), a difficult text to refute:

This passage has on various accounts occasioned so much trouble, that some have not hesitated to alter the punctuation, as if it had been written, "I say unto thee today"; that is, although I seem to-day the most despised and miserable of all men, yet I declare to thee and assure thee, that thou shalt hereafter be with me in paradise, that is, in some pleasant place (for properly speaking paradise is not heaven), or in the spiritual state allotted to the soul and body.[23]

This curious interpretation is also advanced by the Socinian Smalcius,[24] who says that the phrase is a Hebrew manner of speaking (*est loquendi modus Hebraicus*) and repunctuates the quotation in the same way as Milton:

Verba enim Christi, Amen, *dico tibi hodie mecum eris in Paradyso*, ita distingui possunt, *Dico tibi hodie, mecum eris in Paradyso*, ita ut Christus non tempus indicet, quando futurus sit secum in Paradyso latro, sed veritatem ejus, quod promittebat exprimat.[25]

Stegmann[26] who cites Smalcius on Luc.23:43 in his *Photinianismus*,[27] elaborates his point:

Quando vero futurus esset in Paradiso latro ille, id aliunde colligendum esse, nempe, ut ipse latro perierat, cum Christus venturus esset in regno suo, (sic enim habet Graecus textus). Hoc autem futurum est in die ultimo, in quem omnibus aliis fidelibus, quotquotsunt excepto Christo, reposita est ipsorum merces.[28]

Smalcius's refutation of Philippians 1:23 (For I am in a strait betwixt two, having a desire to depart, and to be with Christ; which is far better:) is more consistent with Milton's original argument than is Milton's own treatment of the passage. Milton says:

The fourth text is Philipp.i.23. "having a desire to depart (*cupiens dissolvi*, having a desire for dissolution) and to be with Christ." But, to say nothing of the uncertain and disputed sense of the word ἀναλῦσαι, which signifies anything rather than "dissolution," it may be answered, that although Paul desired to obtain immediate possession of heavenly perfection and glory, in like manner as every one is desirous of attaining as soon as possible to that, whatever it may be, which he regards as the ultimate object of his being, it by no means follows that, when the soul of each individual leaves the body, it is received immediately either into heaven or hell. For he "had a desire to be with Christ"; that is, at his appearing, which all the believers hoped and expected was then at hand.[29]

Smalcius however denies that the soul is even implied in the passage and treats Paul as the whole man: "Sed Paulus nihil de anima loquitur, nec de anima eum loqui, ulla ratione probari potest. Sed de se toto loquitur, quod cupiat esse cum Christo, quaemomodum totus dissolvi cupiebat."[30]

There are other interesting similarities between Milton's treatment of the intermediate state and that of Smalcius.[31] Certainly, Smalcius is very close to Milton in tone when he argues:

Animas sanctorum restare post mortem credimus. Redit enim spiritus hominis, teste S. Scriptura, ad Deum, qui eum dedit. *Sed quia animam istam vel spiritum hominis post mortem aliquid sentire, vel aliqua re perfrui, nec ratio permittit, nec scriptura testatur.*[32]

The commentary of the Socinian Crellius on I Corinthians 5.6,[33] far too lengthy to be quoted here, also contains expressions of Milton's whole man conception; but this instance—like the observations of Smalcius—is only of interest as a comparison, for Milton's basic argument, unlike all others, is based upon, and begins with, the mortality of the soul (the whole man) rather than the sleep of the soul and the problem of the intermediate state. Whatever exegetical data on the matter he may have noticed, his own development of the doctrine, by its fundamental dependence upon his rendition of what he considered the key word (נפש) in Scripture for the whole problem, was most likely, as he himself professed, a result of his free declaration of the true doctrine from the evidence of Scripture alone.

But there is one other figure, that of a great theologian, whose attitude toward the intermediate state is of particular interest, not alone because Milton may have known of his position on the subject, but chiefly because unorthodoxy in such a matter has been rarely associated with his name and has been completely disavowed by his followers. It is not widely known today—nor was it, for that matter, in the seventeenth century—that Martin Luther in some of his writings favored the psychopannychian doctrine.

His commentary on Ecclesiastes 9:10 maintains:

Alius locus quod mortui nihil sentiant, nulla enim, inquit, est ibi cogitatio, ars, cognitio, sapientia. Sensit ergo Solomon mortuos omnino dormire et nihil prorsus sentire. Jacent ibi mortui, non numerantes dies vel annos, sed excitati vedebuntur sibi vix momentum dormivisse.[34]

Which is clearly the soul sleep doctrine. Moreover, in 1520 Luther published a defense of forty-one propositions condemned by a Bull of Leo. The twenty-seventh runs thus (stating that it is not in the power of the church or the pope to establish articles of faith or laws for morals or good works):

Permitto tamen quod Papa condat articulos fidei sibi et suis fidelibus, quales sunt, Panem et vinum transubstantiari in sacramento, essentiam Dei nec generare, nec generari,[35] Animam esse formam substantialem humani corporis. Se esse imperatorem mundi, et regum coeli, et Deum terrenum. Animam esse immortalem; et omnia illa infinita portenta in Romano sterquilinio decretorum, ut qualis est ejus fides, tale sit evangelium, tales, et fideles, talis et ecclesia, et [ut] habeant similem labra lactuatam et dignum patella sit operculum.[36]

This sardonic permission of Luther, evidently aimed at papal decrees founded upon scholastic determinations, includes the belief in the immortality of the soul along with the belief in the pope as emperor of the world as equivalent "monstrous opinions" found in the "Roman dunghill of decretals."

Although there existed the defense of Luther's belief in soul sleep written by Tyndale against More,[37] it is much more likely that Milton, if he knew of Luther's attitude on the intermediate state, learned of it from his oft-quoted Sleidanus who plainly stated, "Docet enim Lutheris e sacris literis mortuorum animas quiescere, et iudicii diem supremem expectare."[38]

So too Milton, *e sacris literis*, formed his doctrine of the death of the whole man and the sleep of death until the day of judgment. The only evident resemblance to Luther lies, of course, in the fact of scriptural derivation; but it can, at least, be observed that Milton, in his opposition to the orthodox conception of the intermediate state of the soul, had distinguished company.

In his heretical opinions, mortalist and pantheistic, which he addressed to the learned with the qualification to accept or reject them only by the clear testimony of revelation, Milton has followed strictly his professed Protestant method of adherence to Scripture alone—without recourse to any other judges or interpreters—under the guidance of the Holy Spirit. Indeed, the full title of his treatise, *John Milton, an Englishman, His Christian Doctrine, Compiled from the Holy Scriptures Alone*, is completely indicative of its contents. The results, theologically, are subject to various evaluations, but in terms of his hermeneutics, his independent logical analyses and linguistic proficiency, the stature of Milton as a first rate student of Scripture and a competent Biblical critic is fully established.

Notes

Chapter I

1. It is regrettable that this epoch of scholarship has no Sandys. There are good brief accounts in Charles A. Briggs's *Biblical Study* (New York, 1884) in Frederic W. Farrar's *History of Interpretation* (London, 1886); and in various encyclopedic notices; but there is no historian for the philological movement as such.

2. Although the terms "hermeneutics" and "exegesis" have become practically interchangeable, as used in this study, "hermeneutics" will refer to the theory of Biblical criticism and "exegesis" to the actual practice of textual criticism. Under exegesis, too, I have included the general field of isagogics or Biblical introduction.

3. Cf. G. C. Taylor, *Milton's Use of Du Bartas* (Cambridge, 1934); Frank E. Robbins, *The Hexaemeral Literature* (Chicago, 1912); Grant McColley, *Paradise Lost* (Chicago, 1940); Sister Mary Irma Corcoran, *Milton's Paradise* (Washington, D. C., 1945), and others. The valuable studies in the hexaemeral literature that have appeared in recent years are of great interest to all students of Milton's great epic. Our concern here, however, is with the actual formulation of Milton's own theological beliefs, quite a different matter from literary parallels. While the relationship of the *De Doctrina* to *Paradise Lost* is still a debated question (despite Kelley's fine work), there can be no doubt that Milton's solemn treatise on theology is the most valid expression of his actual doctrinal convictions.

4. *Infra*, Chapter II.

5. *Infra*, Chapters II, V, and VI. In rational criticism of Scripture, hermeneutics, sectarian tolerance, antitrinitarianism, materialism, and mortalism, the Socinians are not far from Milton.

6. *De Doctrina*, Columbia Edition XIV, 15. The Holy Spirit is Milton's only acknowledged guide. Cf. *ibid.*, XVI, 261, 269.

7. There is also a distinction to be made between Milton's polemical quotations of the Bible in his tracts and pamphlets and the formal exegetical citations of the *De Doctrina*. In the first case, in accordance with the custom of the period, the usage was primarily for authoritative illustration, but in the latter the scriptural passages were cited as integral with the derivation of doctrine. Harris Fletcher's *The Use of the Bible in Milton's Prose* (Urbana, Ill., 1929) is a very useful reference as a digest of the Biblical quotations in Milton's prose works.

8. Maurice Kelley, *This Great Argument* (Princeton, 1941). Although our concern is with the *De Doctrina* and not *Paradise Lost*, Mr. Kelley's excellent study of the *De Doctrina* as "a document indispensable for an appreciation of Milton's art and an understanding of the great argument that he labored to assert in the poetry of *Paradise Lost*," a study which, in my opinion, was completely successful, emphasizes one point in connection with it that should be mentioned here. In his competent refutation of Saurat, Mr. Kelley criticizes Saurat's synthesis as a misleading exposition of Milton's views by saying, "It represents Milton as too abstract a thinker and divorces him from the Bible, with which the Protestant theologian must work." And again in his conclusion, as against the "New Movement" in Milton criticism, Mr. Kelley wisely remarks:

"Behind *Paradise Lost* and its high argument is an aetiological explanation of the problem of evil which is Christian, Protestant, and seventeenth century to the core: Christian in its acceptance of the Hebraic explanation, Protestant in its reliance on the Bible and the Spirit alone, and seventeenth century in its dogged assertion of independency and the dignity of the common man."

A conclusion that seems to be thoroughly demonstrated by Milton's Biblical criticism.

9. Clive S. Lewis, *A Preface to Paradise Lost* (London, 1943) Despite otherwise worth-while criticism, Mr. Lewis, apparently not familiar with Kelley's work, in criticizing the now generally discarded views of Saurat (though he curiously accepts the *Zohar* thesis) seems to feel that because *Paradise Lost* has been ac-

cepted as orthodox by many generations of acute readers well grounded in theology, any prominent notice of Milton's heresies is mistaken criticism. For critical treatment of *Paradise Lost* as Augustinian, hierarchical, and Catholic, Milton's heresies are doubtless inconvenient; facts frequently are.

10. *Ex ipsa Dei scriptura . . . . diligentissime perlecta atque perpensa. De Doctrina,* C.E., XIV, 4.

11. *Summoque solatio fuit, magnum me, Deo bene iuvante subsidium fidei mihimet comparasse. Ibid.,* XIV, 9.

12. For a study of similarities of structure and phrasing in Wolleb and Milton, cf. Maurice Kelley, "Milton's Debt to Wolleb's *Compendium Theologiae Christianae," Publications of the Modern Language Association,* L(1935), 156–65. Milton's own statement of his use of the shorter systems of divines (*De Doctrina,* C.E., XIV, 4) is adequate evidence of his familiarity with them, but by no means indicates a dependency upon them for his theological conceptions. In fact, Milton insists in his Preface, *"De me, libris tantummodo sacris adhaeresco." De Doctrina, ibid.,* XIV, 14.

13. I.e., the Socinians. The sobriquet of "Polish Brethren" (a designation preferred by Socinians) derives from the fact that Poland was the chief seat of their activity. The great corpus of outstanding Socinian works was the famous *Bibliotheca Fratrum Polonorum.*

14. Sometimes wrongly confused with psychopannychism. Psychopannychism, a milder form of mortalism, was the doctrine of the sleep of the soul. Milton holds that the soul dies, not sleeps, and, like the teachers of Arabia combatted by Origen, he refers to the intermediate state as the sleep of death for both body and soul. Cf. K. R. Hagenbach, *A Text-Book of the History of Doctrines* (New York, 1865), I, 217, II, 129.

15. Denis Saurat in his *Milton, Man and Thinker* (New York, 1925), so characterizes Milton's *ex Deo* conception of matter. Saurat maintains that Milton probably drew heavily upon the *De Macrocosmi Historia* of Robert Fludd for this idea. In fact, in a now memorable summary, Saurat maintained that, roughly speaking, the whole of Milton's philosophy is found in the Kabbalah except for his materialism which derives from Fludd and his mortalism which is connected with the ideas of seven-

teenth-century English Mortalists. (*Op. cit.*, p. 280). This sensational conclusion as to Milton's philosophy, long since ignored by scholars, while stimulating, failed primarily because of a fundamental oversight, namely, that Milton was a Puritan, a logician, and, whatever else, assuredly no theosophist. As for his materialism, the mystic Fludd is no more suitable than the *Sefer Zohar*; concerning which, as well as the mortalism, cf. *infra*, Chapters V and VI.

16. I.e., in exegetical derivation.

17. Also Christian Orientalists, infra pp. 20–22.

18. Cf. Harris Fletcher, *Milton's Rabbinical Readings* (Urbana, Ill., 1930).

19. The *Doctrine and Discipline of Divorce.*

20. Particularly interesting in light of Milton's usual scorn for the rabbis. However, the fact that he frequently so alludes to them need be of no consequence in determining their possible role in the formulation of Milton's beliefs. The polemic style of the pamphlets can in no wise be evaluated with the formal theology of the *De Doctrina.*

21. Inasmuch, however, as Milton's doctrinal convictions are manifest in *Paradise Lost* it is necessary to investigate the whole thesis of the rabbinical borrowings. Recent work (*vide supra, n. 3*) indicates that Milton's own wide readings may account for much of the extrabiblical material in the poem; it has yet to be proved, *mi crede*, that *Paradise Lost* is, instead, a mine of rabbinic lore.

22. Nicholaus de Lyra (d. 1340), a converted Jew, was the only exegete of the medieval church who was manifestly familiar with the Hebrew text of the Old Testament. Although formally recognizing the fourfold sense, he showed a marked preference for the literal. He was deeply influenced by the grammatical commentaries of Rashi (Rabbi Salomon ben Isaac, *ca.* 1040–1105), so much so, indeed, that he was dubbed "Rashi's Ape." De Lyra's influence on Luther has been commemorated by the couplet,

> Si Lyra non lyrasset
> Lutherus non saltasset.

23. The revival of classical scholarship was the immediate

forerunner of sacred philology. The stimulus to the study of Greek brought about an interest in the Greek Fathers, the study of Christian antiquity, and the rise of historical investigation. Through the Council of Florence (1439) a large number of Eastern scholars came into Italy; notable of this group were Bessarion, Gemistos Plethon, Theodore of Gaza, and Argyropulos of Constantinople, this last a translator of Aristotle and the instructor of Reuchlin.

24. By his celebrated *De falso credita et ementita Constantini donatione declamatio* (1439).

25. Reuchlin's famous grammar and lexicon, *De Rudimentis Hebraicis*, was actually preceded by the less elaborate Hebrew grammar of Conrad Pellicanus. In 1516 Erasmus edited and published the first edition of the Greek Testament.

26. In the later editions of his New Testament, Erasmus consulted the Complutensian Polyglot which, although actually printed in 1517, was not published until 1522.

27. Johannes Reuchlin (1455-1522), the father of Humanism in Germany, considered the St. Jerome of his day (*eruditio trilinguis*) and celebrated in literature for his connection with the *Epistolae Obscurorum Virorum* (1515), besides his great services to philology and Hebrew studies in Europe, is also of interest as a cabalist. Cf. Joseph L. Blau, *The Christian Interpretation of the Cabala in the Renaissance* (New York, 1944).

28. Canon Farrar, for one, considers Erasmus second only to Luther in widening the knowledge of Scripture and advancing the cause of the Reformation. Cf. Frederic W. Farrar, *History of Interpretation* (London, 1886).

29. *Novum Testamentum omne, diligenter ab Erasmo Roterdamo recognitum et Emandatum* (Basel, 1516).

30. Cf. Farrar, *op. cit.*, p. 318.

31. As well as from Bugenhagen, Jonas, and Cruciger.

32. Philipp Melancthon (1497-1560), author of the *Augsberg Confession* (1530) and first to systematize the reformed theology in his famous *Loci communes rerum theologicarum* (1521), was Luther's great lieutenant.

33. Milton S. Terry, *Biblical Hermeneutics* (New York, 1883), p. 674.

34. Farrar, *op. cit.*, p. 341.

35. Conrad Pellicanus (1478–1556), Professor of Greek and Hebrew at Zurich, was the author of a huge commentary on the Bible (7 vols.; Zurich, 1532–39). His exegesis is particularly good on questions of text, and his critical method was historical. His Hebrew grammar, published in 1503, was the first Hebrew grammar written by a non-Jew, and the first to be printed in a European tongue.

36. Sebastian Münster (1484–1552), though chiefly famous for his *Cosmographia universalis* (1544), a classic of Renaissance geography, published besides Hebrew grammars the first Chaldean, *Grammatica Chaldaica* (1527). In addition he edited the Hebrew Bible (1534–35) from which he subsequently prepared a new Latin translation with notes, and published two lexicons, *Dictionarium Chaldaicum* (1527) and *Dictionarium trilinguae* [Latin, Greek, and Hebrew] (1530).

37. The supplementary fifth volume to the *Bibliotheca magna rabbinica* (1675–93) of Bartoloccus [the foundation for Wolf's *Bibliotheca Hebraea* (1715–33)] was written by his former pupil Imbonatus, who, in fact, completed and edited the fourth volume after the death of Bartoloccus. This fifth volume, *Bibliotheca latino-hebraica, sive de scriptoribus latinis, qui ex diversis nationibus contra Judaeos vel de re hebraica utcumque scripsere* (1694) contains the following notice of Pellicanus (p. 29):

"Pellicanus (Conradus Rubeaquensis) (Auctor damnatus in Romano Indice librorum prohibitorum) scripsit: 1. Grammaticam Hebraicam. 2. Dict. Hebraicam. 3. Syriacos Onkel, Ionathae, aliorumque Iudaeorum interpretationes omnes, in Latinum transtulit . . . . Praeterea transtulit ex Hebraicis plurium Rabbinorum Commentaria ad literam, Nempe: R. David Kimhi in Genesin, Iosue, Iudicum . . . . Item R. Abraham Aben Ezra in xiv libros canonicos iuxta editionem secundam Danielis Bombergi, R. Salamonis Iarchi Galli in omnes canonicos, R. Levi Ben Gerson in Parabolas Salamonis, in Danielem plurimaque in Iosue, Iudicum . . . . Ordinarium Glossam in totum pentateuchum, dictum Berescith Rabba, magnae apud Judaeos auctoritatis. Talmudica quoque in latine reddidit. Pleraque alia scripsit, et transtulit quae offeruantur in Bibliotheca Tigurina [Zurich]."

38. Cf. his preface to Romans.

39. Harris Fletcher, *The Use of the Bible in Milton's Prose*, pp. 50–51.

40. Such as Osiander, Piscator, Bullinger, Chemnitz; cf. Farrar, *op. cit.*, pp. 342 ff.

41. The Antwerp Polyglot (1568–73) was an expansion of the Complutensian (the first of the polyglots completed under Cardinal Ximenes in 1517) prepared under the supervision of Arias Montanus; the Nuremberg (1599–1600) prepared under Elias Hutter had its New Testament in twelve languages.

42. The final expression of medieval exegesis was pronounced at the Council of Trent which insisted that interpretation was limited by these rules: that it must conform to the rule of faith, the canon and authority of the Vulgate, the consent of the Fathers, and the decision of the councils.

43. For a good description of which see Fletcher, *Milton's Rabbinical Readings*, pp. 57 ff.

44. Elias Levita (1469–1549), one of the greatest Jewish scholars of any period, of all his writings is most famous for his *Massoreth Hamasoreth* (1538). In this important critical history of the Massora, Elias Levita first affirmed the punctuation of the text of the Hebrew Bible to be of late origin.

45. Vocalic subscripts attached to the letters of the consonantal Hebrew alphabet for pronunciation.

46. *Manuale Hebraicum et Chaldaicum* (1602).

47. *Synagoga Judaica* (1603).

48. *Lexicon Hebraicum et Chaldaicum* (1607).

49. *Lexicon Chaldaicum et Syriacum*.

50. *Infra.*

51. Briggs (*op. cit.*, p. 145) cites Brian Walton's refutation of John Owen (who upheld the every iota and tittle from God position) as evidence of the contemporary influence of Cappel.

52. Professor of Oriental Languages at Wittemberg and at Helmstadt (d. 1611).

53. Besides collaborative works, the Dictionary of National Biography lists thirteen separate publications.

54. The work of Salomon Glassius and John Leusden also enjoyed great fame. Glassius's *Philologia Sacra* (1623), though competent in learning, maintained a twofold sense of Scripture,

i.e., the literal and the spiritual or mystical, and represented an early departure from the literal tendency of the Reformation and a countercheck to the current grammatico-historical school. The work of Leusden belongs to the latter half of the century and is thoroughly philological in character.

55. In sharp contrast to Glassius with his spiritual sense.

56. The great Hebrew grammarian Wilhelm Gesenius in his essay on "Biblische einleitung, oder einleitung in die Bibel" considered the *Thesaurus Philologicus* with Leusden's *Philologus Hebraeus* (1656) as the first important steps for a thorough learned and critical treatment of introduction. Cf. *Essays and Dissertations in Biblical Literature, By a Society of Clergymen* (New York 1829), p. 10.

57. *De Doctrina*, C.E., XVI, 274–78.

58. Joseph Justus Scaliger (1540–1604). His *De emendatione temporum* (1583) revolutionized the whole conception of ancient chronology. Scaliger alone laid the foundation for the science of historical criticism.

59. The work of Samuel Bochart (1599–1667) on the geography of the Bible, *Geographia Sacra* (1646), and his treatise on the animals mentioned in Scripture, *Hierozoicon* (1663), enjoyed a fame which was recognized as late as the nineteenth century. His erudition in Arabic led to a visit to Stockholm in 1652 where he studied the Arabic manuscripts of Christina.

60. Constantine L'Empereur (d. 1648), Professor of Hebrew at Leyden, though by no means the equal of Lightfoot in Talmudic studies, by his *Clavis Talmudica* (1634) and his *Talmudis Babylonici Codex Middoth* (1630), the latter in Hebrew and Latin, is recognized as a pioneer in the field.

61. William Schickhard (d. 1635) Professor of Hebrew at Tubingen, was known to Milton (mentioned in the *Commonplace Book*, C.E., XVIII, 186). His studies in Hebrew law were superseded by those of Selden. (*Jus regium Hebraeorum.*) Richard Simon (in his *Histoire Critique du Vieux Testament* [1685], p. 474) bluntly describes Schickhard: "Mais sa méthode est trop Juive, et ne peut pas être utile â toutes sortes de personnes. Il affecte aussi trop de paroître sçavant dans les Livres des Rabbins, quoi qu'il se trompe quelquefois en les traduisant."

62. Gerhard Voss (1577–1649), friend of Grotius and scholar of historical theology, was among the first to treat theological dogmas from a purely historical point of view (especially in his *Historia Pelagiana*, 1618).

63. Ugolinus, *Thesaurus antiquitatum sacrarum complectens selectissima clariss. Virorum opuscula, in quibus Veterum Heraeorum mores, leges, instituta, ritus sacri et civiles illustrantur* (34 vols.; 1744–69). Although containing much that was written in the century of publication, the great majority of the works are by seventeenth-century scholars.

64. *Harmony of the IV Evangelists among Themselves and with the Old Testament, with an Explanation of the Chiefest Difficulties Both in Language and Sense*. Published in three parts at London in 1644, 1647, and 1650.

65. A series of studies first collected together in the complete works in 1684.

66. Excepting, naturally, the great Jewish scholars.

67. Oxford's first professor of Arabic, Pococke made a number of translations from Arabic, most important of which was the *Historia compendiosa dynastiarum* (1663), a translation of Bar Hebraeus.

68. The actual text was Arabic in Hebrew characters.

69. Particularly the *Uxor Ebraica* (1646) although Milton also mentions the *De Diis Syris* and the *De Jure Naturali et Gentium juxta Disciplinam Ebraeorum* (1640).

70. Johannes Cocceius (1603–69), whose conception of a double covenant—the covenant of Works before the Fall and the covenant of Grace after—was part of the Federal School of Theology (which has been described as a soteriology), was the author of a distinguished philological work, *Lexicon et commentarius Hebraici et Chaldaici* (1669).

71. In his *Summa Doctrinae de Foedere et Testamento Dei* (1648), Farrar (*op. cit.*, pp. 385–86) remarks that it "taught his contemporaries to study the structure of the Bible and to abandon the unfruitful method of splitting it into isolated texts." And he concludes: "Unhappily however the good which Cocceius did in one direction he undid in another. He emancipated exegesis from a dull tyranny, but subjected it to an extravagant

typology. He was the first to sanction a system of parallels between the Old and New Testament of which many were purely fanciful."

72. Despite the early *Defensio fidei catholicae de Satisfactione Christi adversus Faustum Socinum* (1617) written by Grotius in refutation of Socinus's *De Jesu Christo Servatore*. His later studies of Socinian works at Paris tended to modify his judgments, and he began to disregard doctrinal differences in favor of general Protestant unity. Accordingly, when in his famous *De Veritate Religionis Christianae* (1627), he defended Christianity on rational grounds and later emphasized the moral quality of the Christian life over mere correctness of belief, despite his disagreement with some points of Socinian doctrine, it can be fairly said that his emphasis was indeed Socinian.

73. Abraham Calov (d. 1686), militant *defensor fidei* of Lutheranism, was the great heresy hunter of the century. His life was devoted to bitter polemics, and he was the Bigot General of his age. Legend describes his daily prayer as *Imple Me, Deus, odio haereticorum.*

74. Hammond, Clericus, Pococke, Whitby, Lowth, *aliosque.*

75. Briggs, *op. cit.*, p. 345.

76. Milton mentions frequently the commentaries of Grotius. For a specific instance, see the passage from the *Doctrine and Discipline of Divorce, infra*, Chap. IV.

77. Johannes Drusius (1550–1616), Professor of Oriental Languages at Oxford (1572–76) and Leyden (1577–85) and Professor of Hebrew at Franeker (1585–1616).

78. Louis de Dieu (1590–1642). His later comments on Acts (1634) included the Ethiopic as well as the Arabic texts.

79. *Biblia Sacra Polyglotta Edidit Brianus Waltonus* (6 vols.; London, 1657). This, the greatest of all the polyglots, was compiled by Walton with the assistance of Pococke, Castell, Thomas Hyde, Lightfoot, Louis de Dieu, and others. Nine languages are included, although no single book includes the full number.

80. *Lexicon Heptaglotton, Hebraicum, Chaldaicum, Syriacum, Samaritanum, Aethiopicum, Arabicum, cunjunctim et Persicum separatim*, (London, 1669), 2 vols. Castell spent eighteen years and the bulk of his fortune (12,000 £) on this huge task. It had a poor sale in his day, despite its great worth, and would quite

likely fare no better in these times. It was specifically written
for use with the London Polyglot.

81. *Critici Sacri, sive annotata doctissimorum virorum in vetus
ac Novum Testamentum, quibus accedunt tractatus varii theologico-
philologici* (London, 1660), 9 vols. Produced under the direction
of Bishop Pearson as an appendage to the London Polyglot. The
Amsterdam edition (1698–1732) has an additional four volumes
of lexicographic material.

82. *Synopsis criticorum aliorumque S. Scripturae interpretum*
(London, 1669–76). Poole's abridgment of the *Critici Sacri* contains a great number of critics not included in the original.
Leusden's edition of the *Synopsis* (1684) is the best of the many
reprints.

83. Fletcher (*Use of the Bible in Milton's Prose*, pp. 87–88)
disagrees with Sumner's decision that Milton's rendering of a
Syriac word derives from an English translation of the Bible and
suggests that the London Polyglot—despite the existence of
earlier translations of the Syriac in separate editions as well as
in the Antwerp Polyglot—was the likelier source, a conclusion
that seems sound in view of Milton's allusion to a recent translation. More conclusive evidence of Milton's acquaintance with
the London Polyglot it seems to me is his allusion to the Ethiopic
text. Milton remarks (*De Doctrina*, C.E., XIV, 214) apropos of
the "spurious passage" in I John 7:

"Praeterquam quod in Syro et duabus reliquis Orientalium
versionibus, Arabica nimirum et Aethiopica, et in plerisque
Graecis codicibus antiquis non reperiatur hic versus . . . . certe
de unitate consensus et testimonii itidem ut loco proxime citato,
duntaxat hic agi ab Ioanne, siquidem Ionnis haec vere sunt, non
vidit modo Erasmus, sed Beza etiam vel invitus agnovit."

The textual inaccuracy of this famous passage had been frequently noted. In view of its bearing on the question of the
Trinity, it is not surprising to see that the Racovian Catechism
practically paraphrases Milton's remarks:

"What answer do you make to the third testimony quoted
from the First Epistle of John, respecting the three heavenly
witnesses?

"I observe, first, that since it is known that these words are
wanting *in most of* the older Greek copies, and also in the

Syriac, Arabic, Aethiopic, and the more ancient Latin versions, as the principal persons even among our adversaries have themselves shown, nothing can be concluded from them. There are, besides, some persons who deem the genuineness of the passage suspicious; that is to say, Erasmus, Beza, Franc. Lucas, and the Louvain divines."

From the Racovian Catechism, tr. and ed. by Thomas Rees (London, 1818), Chap. I, Sec. III.

According to Rees, the original of the Racovian Catechism was here amended to *plerisque* (Milton's word too, incidentally) because Erasmus found the words ["there are three," etc.] in the *Codex Britannicus* and Stephanus also found them in a few manuscripts. (This *Codex Britannicus* is really the *Codex Dublinensis* written in 1520. It contains the disputed passage, but poorly translated, from the Vulgate. It is certain that Erasmus never saw the MS which he notices as the *Codex Britannicus*. An extract was sent to him containing the verse, and on this authority he inserted it in the third edition of his Greek Testament.)

Despite the occurrence of Milton's argument in the Racovian Catechism, since he very probably would have shunned a secondary source on so vital a problem, it is almost certain that Milton's textual information came from the London Polyglot. Although an edition of the Ethiopic New Testament appeared in 1548 (cf. Jacques Le Long, *Bibliotheca Sacra* [Antwerp, 1709], I, Part II, 152, for a description of this version), there is no evidence that Milton knew Ethiopic. In the London Polyglot there was available the first Latin translation of the Ethiopic text as well as "the other two Oriental versions," and in Volume VI there were listed the variant readings of the various Greek manuscripts.

84. C.E., XVIII, 306.

85. *Ubi quam plurimus qui vulgo finguntur Hebraismis larva detrahitur*, as Pfochen describes his work.

86. Gataker was a distinguished Greek scholar in his own right. Cf. John Edwin Sandys, *A History of Classical Scholarship* (Cambridge, 1908), II, 341–42.

87. *The Christian Synagogue, Wherein Is Contained the Diverse Reading, the Right Poynting, Translation, and Collation of*

Scripture with Scripture. With the Customs of the Hebrewes and Proselytes and of All Those Nations with Whom They Were Conversant (London, 1623). The possible importance of Weemse to the Milton student has been mentioned by Fletcher, Corcoran, and others.

88. Numerous editions of the Hebrew text of the Bible with literal sublinear translations and, even, transliterations of the Hebrew appeared in the seventeenth century.

89. Hugh Cressy (as an interesting instance) in his *Exomologesis* (London, 1647), (pp. 178–79) says he heard Ussher say that he had intended to publish the New Testament in Greek with various "lections and annotations," but gave it up because he was afraid the number of notes and versions "should rather have made men atheistically to doubt of truth of the whole book than satisfy them in the true reading of any particular passage."

Chapter II

1. *Westminster Confession*, I (Of the Holy Scripture):
4) "The authority of the Holy Scripture, for which it ought to be believed and obeyed, dependeth not upon the testimony of any man or church, but wholly upon God, (who is truth itself,) the author thereof: and therefore it is to be received, because it is the word of God."

The authority of the Church can only induce a high and reverent esteem for the Holy Scripture and "the full discovery it makes of the only way of man's salvation," but "the assurance of the infallible truth . . . . is from the inward work of the Holy Spirit." (I, 5)

And for interpretation and resolution of doctrine:
9) "The infallible rule of interpretation of Scripture is the Scripture itself, and therefore, when there is a question about the true and full sense of any Scripture (which is not manifold, but one), it must be searched and known by other places that speak more clearly."

10) "The supreme judge, by which all controversies of religion are to be determined and all decrees of councils, opinions of ancient writers, doctrines of men, and private spirits are to be examined, and in whose sentence we are to rest, can be no other but the Holy Spirit, speaking in the Scripture."

2. The best account by far is in Tulloch's *Rational Theology and Christian Philosophy in England in the Seventeenth Century* (Edinburgh, 1874), I, 261–343.

3. *The Works of William Chillingworth, M.A.* (Oxford, 1838), II, 410.

4. *Ibid.*, pp. 37–38.

5. *Ibid.*, I, 166–70.

6. *Ibid.*, II, 411.

7. ". . . . following the Scripture, I shall believe many mysteries, but no impossibilities; many things above reason, but nothing against it . . . . Nay, I shall believe nothing which reason will not convince that I ought to believe it: for reason will convince any man, unless he be of perverse mind, that the scripture is the word of God: and then no reason can be greater than this: God says so, therefore it is true." *Ibid.*, p. 413.

8. *Ibid.*, I, 14–15.

9. *Ibid.*, pp. 236–38.

10. *Ibid.*, pp. 235–36.

11. *Ibid.*, pp. 231–33.

12. A. Barker in his *Milton and the Puritan Dilemma* (Toronto, 1942), p. 244, for instance, has noticed the similarity between them in their conception of heresy.

13. Typical, by way of direct contrast with *The Religion of Protestants*, is Matthew Poole's *A Dialogue between a Popish Priest and an English Protestant* (London, 1685).

14. John Ball, *A Short Treatise Containing All the Principall Grounds of Christian Religion* (10th impression; London, 1635), p. 39. Ball is also quoted by Briggs who remarks (*Bibical Study* pp. 336–37) that Ball's conception that the analogy of faith is expressly "set downe in plainer places of Scripture" and that the Holy Ghost is the only faithful interpreter, was an important improvement of the Protestant principle since by qualifying it as the Holy Spirit speaking directly through the word to the believer it prevented the substitution of an external symbol or system of theology for the rule of faith of the Scriptures.

15. Goodwin, John, *Divine Authority of the Scriptures Asserted*, p. 16.

16. Francis Roberts in his *Key of the Bible* (4th ed.; London), pp. 5 ff., recommends as special and peculiar rules for scholars:

1. The competent understanding of the original languages
2. The prudent use of Logick
3. The subservient help of other arts, as Rhetoric, Natural Philosophy, etc.
4. The benefit of humane histories to illustrate and clear the theme.
5. The conferring of ancient translations with the originals.
6. The prudent use of the most orthodox, learned, and judicious Commentators.

As against the more general and common directions for "Christians of all sorts, learned and unlearned":

1. Beg wisdom of the onely wise God.
2. Labor sincerely after a truly gracious spirit.
3. Peruse the Scripture with an humble self-denying heart.
4. Familiarize the Scripture to thyself by constant and methodical exercise therein.
5. Understand Scripture according to the theological analogy or certain rule of faith and love.

17. John Owen (1616–83), who ranks with Baxter and Howe in prominence, was one of the most learned of the Puritan divines.

18. *The Reason of Faith; or, An Answer to That Enquiry, Wherefore We Believe the Scripture To Be the Word of God* (originally published in 1677). I have used a nineteenth-century edition, Glasgow, 1801, pp. 288–94.

19. Owen, *op. cit.*, p. 297.

20. *Ibid.*, pp. 297–98.

21. "Verum cum aeternae salutis viam non nisi propriae cuiusque fidei, Deus aperuerit, postuletque hoc a nobis, ut qui salvus esse vult, pro se quisque credat, statui divinis in rebus, non aliorum niti vel fide vel iudicio, sed quid credendum in religione est, id fide non aliunde quam divinitus accepta, et quod mearum erat partium non omisso, ex ipsa Dei scriptura quam diligentissime perlecta atque perpensa, unumquodque habere mihimet ipsi, meaque ipsius opera exploratum atque cognitum." *De Doctrina*, C.E., XIV, 4.

22. "Coepi igitur Adolescens .... cum ad libros utriusque Testamenti lingua sua perlegendos assiduus incumbere, tum Theologorum Systemata aliquot breviora sedulo percurrere: ad

eorum deinde exemplum, locos communes digerere, ad quos omnia quae ex scripturis haurienda occurrissent, ex promenda cum opus esset, referrem. Ad uberiora deinde Theologorum volumina et disputatas in utramque partem de capitibus quibusdam fidei quaestiones, fidentius demum me contuli: liceat candide non minus quam libere dicam, multa ibi adversariorum argumenta misere elusa, aut elenchorum ostentatis putide formulis aut interiectis ubique Grammaticorum inanibus vocabulis in speciem potius quam solide refutata, sane dolens, reperi: . . . . Cum itaque his ducibus neque summam fidei neque spem salutis posse me recte committere arbitrarer . . . . nihil mihi tutius neque consultius visum est, quam ut ipse aliquid huiusmodi quod ad manum mihi esset, labore ac lucubratione propria ex ipso adeoque solo Deo verbo . . . . de integro componerem." *Ibid.*, pp. 4–6.

23. "De me, libris tantummodo sacris adhaeresco; haeresin aliam, sectam aliam sequor nullam; haereticorum, quos vocant, libros perlegeram nullos, cum ex eorum numero, qui orthodoxi audient, re male gesta scripturisque incautius tractatis, sentire cum adversariis quoties illi sentiebant cum scripturis primo didici." *Ibid.*, p. 14.

24. *Ibid.*, XVI, 248–84.

25. *Paradise Lost*, XII, 509–14.

26. "Humanae autem traditiones sive scriptae sive non scriptae palam prohibentur." *De Doctrina*, C.E., XVI, 280.

27. "Qui igitur fidelibus, quorum unusquisque Dei spiritu regitur, sanctiones quascunque suas et dogmata sive ecclesiae, sive Christiani magistratus nomine invitis imposuerit, is non hominibus tantum, verum etiam ipso sancto spiritui iugum imponit." *Ibid.*, XVI, 280.

28. *Ibid.*, XIV, 16.

29. "Haec igitur doctrina, non ex philosophantium scholis, neque ex humanis legibus, sed ex sacris duntaxat literis, praeunte sancto spiritui, petenda est." *Ibid.*, p. 18.

30. Says Mr. Fletcher (*Milton's Rabbinical Readings*, p. 304):
"However we need to recognize clearly that Milton was never being particularly original when he did this [disregarding the plain sense of a passage] but was almost invariably depending upon the original reading or some commentator whom he had read. It was difficult even three centuries ago to suggest new

meanings for the text of Scripture. In his use of the Bible in the *De Doctrina*, Milton's greatest inconsistency is more apparent than real. He was honest enough in stating that he was going to set forth a system of theology based *solely* on Scripture. But for a man who had read as much critical Biblical material as he had, such a procedure was actually impossible, although he himself may have been and no doubt really was completely unaware of the fact."

This insight of Mr. Fletcher as to the inner processes of Milton's mind is, of course, particularly convenient for his later conclusion (*Milton's Rabbinical Readings*, pp. 310–11) that "his interpretation of Scripture often reflects very strongly his reading of rabbinical commentaries."

31. *De Doctrina*, C.E., XIV, 6–7.

32. "Perspicuae itaque sunt scripturae, vel per se, vel Deo illuminante; in iis quae maxime ad salutem pertinent, et ad imperitos perdiligentiam lectionemque assiduam erudiendos accomodatae." *Ibid.*, XVI, 258.

33. "Quid hoc insaniae est, reformatos etiam, sanctissima religionis capita quasi in sacris libris obscurius tradita, ex metaphysicorum densissimis tenebris explanare." *Ibid.*, p. 260.

34. *Ibid.*, p. 254.

35. "Ratio recte interpretandi scripturas utilius quidem a Theologis traditur, quam diligentius aut fidelius observatur; linguarum peritia; fontium inspectio; scopi animadversio; locutionis propriae et figuratae distinctio; causarum, circumstantiarum, antecedentium, consequentium consideratio; locorum cum aliis locis comparatio; fidei quoque analogia ubique spectanda est; syntaxeos denique haud raro anomalia non omittenda . . . . Postremo, ex iis quae scripta sunt, nulla consectaria, nisi necessario plane deducta sunt admittenda." *Ibid.*, p. 262–64.

36. *Supra*, Chap. I, *n.* 83.

37. "Scriptura enim externa, praesertim novi testamenti, ut de supposititiis nihil dicam . . . . scriptura inquam novi testamenti, cum sub custodibus variis male fidendis, ex manuscriptis proinde variis et discrepantibus, varie quoque descripta et excusa demum sit; saepe corrumpi potuit, et corrupta est." *De Doctrina*, C.E., XVI, 274.

38. *Ibid.*, p. 276.

39. *Ibid.*, p. 278. "Utcunque scripturis generatim et universim quidem creditur, primo propter auctoritatem sive ecclesiae visibilis sive codicum manuscriptorum; postea vero ecclesiae ipsisque codicibus eorumque singulis partibus propter auctoritatem totius scripturae secum collatae; toti denique scripturae propter ipsum spiritum unicuique fidelium intus persuadentem."

40. *Ibid.*, XIV, 196.

41. In his *Religious Thought in England* (London, 1870), pp. 191–95.

42. The Socinians made the authority of Scripture subordinate to that of reason. Cf.:

[1] Otto Fock, *Der Socinianismus* (Kiel, 1847), pp. 291 ff.

[2] E. M. Wilbur, *A History of Unitarianism* (Harvard, 1946), pp. 264, 586.

[3] K. R. Hagenbach, *A Textbook of the History of Doctrines* (New York, 1865), pp. 239–40.

43. Fock, *op. cit.*, pp. 291–413.

44. Socinian, so-called from Raków (the place of publication of the first edition [in Polish], 1605), at which the Socinians established their college and held their synods. An excellent account of the Racovian Catechism can be found in Wilbur, *op. cit.*, Chap. XXXI.

45. Wilbur, *op. cit.*, p. 412.

46. *Ibid.*

47. Simon Episcopius (1583–1643), Professor of Divinity at Leyden, was expelled by the Synod of Dort (1618) for his Arminianism (which he actually learned from Arminius, his friend). He was a scholar of considerable learning and influenced numerous later theologians.

48. Partially, as Glass and Cocceius, or wholly, as Boehme.

49. *Supra, n.* 31.

50. *De Doctrina*, C.E., XIV, 14.

51. *Ibid.*, p. 8 "Haec, quibus, melius aut pretiosius nihil habeo."

52. *Ibid.*, XVI, 266.

Chapter III

1. "There was not in the whole university, I believe, a more expert, a more cultured, or a nobler Latinist than Milton,

whether in prose or in verse."—David Masson, *Life of John Milton* (New York, 1946), I, 208.

2. Phillips in his *Life of Milton* (1694) besides enumerating the Greek and Latin texts used by his tutor Milton adds:

"Nor did the time thus studiously employed in conquering the Greek and Latin tongues hinder the attaining to the chief Oriental languages, viz., the Hebrew, Chaldee, and Syriack, so far as to go through the Pentateuch, or five books of Moses in Hebrew, to make a good entrance into the Targum or Chaldee Paraphrase, and to understand several chapters of St. Mathew in the Syriack Testament . . . . and into the Italian and French tongues ["at any odd hour" as Milton suggested in *Of Education*] by reading in Italian Giovan Villani's History . . . . and in French a great part of Pierre Davity."

3. Masson, *op. cit.*, p. 208.

4. James Bass Mullinger in his *Cambridge Characteristics in the Seventeenth Century* (London, 1867), pp. 56–57, while deploring the general level of Cambridge classical scholarship in the earlier part of the century, pointedly excuses Milton (along with Meric Casaubon, Herbert, Barrow, and DuPort) from the charge of not possessing "that refined form of scholarship represented in the present day [Mr. Mullinger, need I say, is speaking of the last century] by so nice a sense of the beauties and delicacies of Greek and Latin verse." He adds that Milton, indeed, stood in painful contrast to his university with his superiority in classical studies.

5. John Edwin Sandys, *A History of Classical Scholarship* (Cambridge, 1908), II, 347.

6. *Ibid.*, p. 345.

7. "And when the Gentiles heard this, they were glad, and glorified the word of the Lord: and as many as were ordained to eternal life believed." (A. V.)

ἀκούντα δὲ τὰ ἔθνη ἔχαιρον καὶ ἐδόξαζον τὸν λόγον τοῦ κυρίου, καὶ ἐπίστευσαν ὅσοι ἦσαν τεταγμένοι εἰς ζωὴν αἰωνιον

This passage has a consistent history of exegetical controversy.

8. *De Doctrina*, C.E., XIV, 124–26.

9. *Ibid.*, p. 130.

10. "Quocirca sagaciores meo quidem iudicio interpretes aliquam in verbo graeco τεταγμένοι quod *ordinati* vertitur

subesse ambiguitatem existimant, et idem valere τεταγμένοι, quod εὖ ἤτοι μετρίως διατεθειμένοι, bene aut mediocriter dispositi sive affecti, animo composito, attento, erecto, et non inordinato; contra atque illi Iudaei fuerunt, ad vitam aeternam, qui sermonem Dei repulerant, seque indignos vita aeterna ostenderant. Significatio affinis huius vocis *Ordinati* inusitata Graecis non est; ut apud Plutarchum in Pompeio." *Ibid.*, p. 128.

11. Who remarks: τεταγμένοι *Hi opponuntur eis, qui se ea vita indignos judicaverunt* i.e., ostenderant. inter alia significat parare. (Ad Acta Apostolorum 13:48 Annotationes in Novum Testamentum, 1644).

12. Hammond notes Mead's exegesis with approval and elaborates on τεταγμένοι for two whole folio pages. He concludes, "The short is, that they having renounced the heathen Idols of their countries embraced the worship of the one only true God, and the hope of eternal life, and so were . . . . well placed or disposed, in a good posture toward the kingdom of God" and finally adds a long postscript to prove "that this phrase cannot reasonably be interpreted to any sense of divine predestination." (*Paraphrase and Annotations on the New Testament* [London, 1653].

13. F. Socinus, *Praelectiones Theologicae* (Amsterdam, 1656) [Vol. I of the *Bibliotheca Fratrum Polonorum*], p. 555.

14. T. Rees, *The Racovian Catechism* (London, 1818), p. 343: "What do you say to the third testimony [Acts xii–48]?

"That this testimony does not take away free will may be perceived from hence,—that no mention is made here of God, who had ordained these persons to eternal life; but it is merely written that "as many as were ordained to eternal life, believed": which may be understood of some ordination made by the men themselves; as if he had said, As many as had ordained themselves, or as many as were fit, from the probity of their minds to embrace the doctrine of Christ."

15. Cf. Mullinger, *op. cit.*, p. 88; Masson, *op. cit.*, p. 124; and Harris Fletcher, *Milton's Semitic Studies* (Chicago, 1926), pp. 54–60.

16. Both Mead and Milton emphasize that the Acts passage is primarily contrasting, not the elect with the damned, but the damned with each other. Paul is arguing, they say, that the

Jews blasphemed and the rest of the Gentiles were not fit. Only
the proselytes, those disposed and fit to believe, believed. Cf.
The Works of the Pious and Profoundly-Learned Joseph Mede,
B.D. (4th ed.; London, 1677), pp. 20 ff. (He always wrote his
name "Mead." The form "Mede" is doubtless an editorial adap-
tion of the latinized "Medus.") Cf. also *De Doctrina,* C.E.,
XIV, 128.

17. Mead, *op. cit.,* p. 21.

18. Budé, ΛΕΞΙΚΟΝ ΕΛΛΗΝΟΡΩ (Basel, 1568). Estienne
["Henry ii"], *Thesaurus Linguae Graecae* (Geneva, 1572),
Vol. III.

19. *Of Education,* C.E., IV, 285.

20. A good account of the St. Paul's School curriculum is
given in Fletcher, *Milton's Semitic Studies,* pp. 32–41, and he
includes an interesting sketch of Milton's tutors, pp. 49–60.
For a fuller account, cf., Mullinger's *History of the University
of Cambridge* (London, 1888), Vol. II, F. Watson, *The English
Grammar Schools to 1660* (Cambridge, 1908) and the definitive
study, D. L. Clark, *Milton at St. Paul's School* (New York, 1948).

Pool's article on "Hebrew Learning among the Puritans of
New England prior to 1700" (*Publications of the American Jewish
Historical Society,* No. 20, 1911, pp. 31–83), while concerned
with New England, contains some reflections on the Hebrew
learning of seventeenth-century Oxford and Cambridge that are
of interest.

For instance, as to the existence of Jewish tutors:

"For academic Hebrew learning that flourished indigenously
in the sequestered cloisters of Oxford and Cambridge, often
under the care of converted Jews, could not thrive so fruitfully
in the ruder atmosphere of the colony." (p. 35).

And as to the general level of training in the universities:

"We must remember that a modicum of Hebrew knowledge
was the common possession of every university-trained cleric of
the time; and although this knowledge was in some cases, such
as in the men who prepared the Authorized Version of 1611,
very considerable, in the majority of cases it must have been
conventionally fragmentary and rudimentary." (p. 36)

21. M. Kayserling, "Les Hebraisants Chrètiens Du XVIIe
Siécle," *Revue des études Juives,* XX (1890), 263: "La plupart

des hebraisants chrètiens du XVII⁰ siècle se firent instruire par les Juifs."

22. There was no adequate collection of Hebrew books at the Cambridge University Library until 1647. Sixteen years after Milton left the university, the English Parliament purchased the Hebrew library of Isaac Pragius. [Pragius was an incorrect transliteration of פראג׳י. The name should be spelled Faraji.] C. E. Sayle remarks of the Bibliotheca Isaaci Pragensi:

"About a year before the transaction which has been discussed in this paper the Senate of the University of Cambridge, by a Grace dated April 4, 1647, thanked Selden for his services with reference to the removal of the Lambeth library to Cambridge. This library contained a good handful of Hebrew books, and though they were subsequently returned, they were still in Cambridge when the Faraji collection arrived. The library also possessed a few Hebrew books from the earlier bequests . . . . But it was the Faraji collection that formed the foundation of the Hebrew library at the University." ("The Purchase of Hebrew Books by the English Parliament in 1647," *Transactions of the Jewish Historical Society* [London, 1915–18].)

23. Louis I. Newman in his *Jewish Influence on Christian Reform Movements* (New York, 1925), p. 99, says of this:

"The third factor in the development of English Hebraic studies was the influence of Jewish commentaries upon Christian exegesis. The works of Rashi, David Kimchi, Ibn Ezra, and other medieval rabbis were made available to Christian scholars, *not so much through the original Hebrew texts, which few Christians, even though well versed in Hebrew, were able to consult* as through the writings of medieval Latinists, among them Nicholas of Lyra, who revealed to the Christian world the commentaries of Rashi; moreover, the editions of Christian Hebraists such as Pagninus, Reuchlin, and others who compiled dictionaries, grammars, and material from the commentaries, placed the works of medieval Jewish exegetes at the command of non-Jewish scholars." (Italics are mine.)

24. C.E., Vol. I.

25. Cf. Fletcher, *Milton's Semitic Studies*, pp. 100–07.

26. Israel Abrahams, *The Book of Delight and Other Papers* (Philadelphia, 1912), pp. 247–50. Abrahams notes, for instance,

that the word *Jimmotu* which appears in the margin is proof that Milton appreciated the force of the *dagesh* and that in the words *shiptu-al* and *bagnadath-el* there is a comparable understanding of the *makkef*.

27. Henry Snyder Gerhard, "Milton's Use of Hebrew in the *De Doctrina Christiana*," *Jewish Quarterly Review*, N.S., XXIX, No. 1, 437–41.

28. Fletcher, *Milton's Rabbinical Readings*, pp. 100 ff.

29. Proverbs 8:27:
When he prepared the heavens, I *was* there: when he set a compass upon the face of the depth.

30. *Paradise Lost*, Book VII, ll. 224–29.

31. Fletcher, *Milton's Rabbinical Readings*, pp. 100–01.

32. מחוגה is the specific word for compasses.

33. Fletcher, *Milton's Rabbinical Readings*, p. 102.

34. S. B. Liljegren, in a caustic review of *Milton's Rabbinical Readings* (*Beiblatt zur Anglia*, XLIII, 377), suggests that the "compass" usage derives from the contemporary pictorial conception of Urania (invoked by Milton in Book VII of *Paradise Lost*) as holding a globe and compasses.

35. *Lexicon Pentaglotton*, p. 534.

36. *Critica Sacra*, p. 70.

37. *Lexicon Chaldaicum Talmudicum et Rabbinicum*, p. 716.

38. *Lexicon Pentaglotton*, p. 535.

39. In his *Annotata Ad Libros Hagiographos sive Criticorum Sacrorum* (1660), III, 4100. Ralph Baynes (d. 1559), Bishop of Lichfield, one of the restorers of Hebrew learning in England, was also the author of two works on Hebrew grammar.

40. *Paradise Lost*, Bk. I, ll. 19–22.

41. *Ibid.*, Bk. VII, ll. 235–37.

42. See especially G. C. Taylor's *Milton's Use of DuBartas* (Cambridge, Mass., 1934). The notion of the impregnation of chaos by the spirit of God, rabbinical though it may appear, is also found in Basil, Jerome, Diodorus of Tarsus, Ambrose, Augustine, Glyca, Honorius, Abelard, Eriugena, Strabus, Angelomus, Procopius, and others. Cf. F. E. Robbins, *The Hexaemeral Literature* (Chicago, 1912), p. 49.

43. Cf. Kelley, *op. cit.*, p. 112, *n.* 74.

44. *De Doctrina*, C.E., XIV, 358–60.

45. *Ibid.*, XV, 12.

ET SPIRITU DEI. Gen 1:2. *Spiritus Dei incubabat, id est virtus potius divina, quam persona aliqua.*

46. *Ibid.*, XIV, 260.

Chapter IV

1. Commenting on the similarities between Gerson's commentary on the eighth chapter of Proverbs and certain ideas of Milton in *Paradise Lost*, Mr. Fletcher observes (*Milton's Rabbinical Readings*, pp. 135-36):

"Wherever else Milton may have encountered such ideas, the rabbis would have determined his use of them.

"For, in dealing with Scripture, Milton had a definite scheme for the gradation of authorities. This is so well known that it is necessary here only to refer to it in order to point out why he drew on rabbinical commentaries as sources. The fact that in dealing with the process or idea of creation he was dealing with scriptural materials, imparted an authority for him to rabbinical commentaries on the text of Scripture which, as in the cases of their actual citations in his prose works, far outweighed in significance the authority as sources of other and more conjectural opinions. Thus the reason for his selection of the particular presentation of the process of creation he adopted . . . . was the fact that he found both of these ideas in the most authentic sources possible next to the text of Scripture itself, in the rabbinical commentaries attached directly to the Hebrew text."

It is this notion of Mr. Fletcher's that especially needs correction. Rabbinical parallels to various figures in *Paradise Lost* are interesting as such, but the idea of the authoritative role (second only to Scripture) of rabbinical commentaries in Milton's thought—particularly in so theological a matter as creation—cannot bear examination.

2. Fletcher, *Milton's Rabbinical Readings*, p. 45.

3. Rashi (R. Solomon ben Isaac) (*ca.* 1040-1105), was the best known to Christian Europe of all the great Jewish exegetes. His commentary on the Pentateuch, printed at Reggio in 1475, was the first dated Hebrew book in print. His fame rests largely upon his exegetical glosses to the Bible and to the Talmud. They

are not, however, consecutive commentaries, but detached glosses on difficult words and phrases. The primary characteristic of Rashi's glosses was clarity.

Abraham ben Meir Ibn Ezra (1093–1167), poet, philosopher, and exegete, was the greatest of the medieval Biblical commentators. Through his knowledge of Arabic, he was the first scholar to disseminate the culture embodied in the Biblical lore of the countries influenced by Mohammedan civilization.

Levi ben Gerson (Ralbag) (1288–1344), scientist and philosopher, was the most versatile of the medieval rabbis. His works show a high degree of linguistic attainment. He wrote a treatise on the telescope, and supported himself by practicing medicine. His greatest work, *Milhamot Adonai* (Wars of the Lord), was highly philosophical in nature. It is a pity that so great a figure is not more widely known.

David Kimchi (d. 1240) was a noted grammarian as well as an exegete. Throughout the later Middle Ages his commentaries were highly respected by both Jews and Christians, and portions of them were translated into Latin.

4. *An Apology against a Pamphlet Call'd a Modest Confutation of the Animadversions of the Remonstrant against Smectymnuus,* C.E., III, Part I, 315–16.

5. Numbers 25:8. "And he went after the man of Israel into the tent, and thrust both of them through, the man of Israel, and the woman through her belly."

6. Fletcher, *op. cit.*, p. 23.

7. The original text makes it plain that the A.V.'s "through her belly" for אל קבתה (*in eius vulvam*) is euphemistic.

8. Fletcher, *op. cit.*, pp. 23–24.

9. *Ibid.*, p. 25.

10. *Ibid.*, p. 26.

11. *Lexicon Pentaglotton.*

12. Fletcher, *op. cit.*, pp. 48–49. Mr. Fletcher quotes the entire title page of Schindler in order, as he puts it, "to give a better idea of the enormous amount of material contained in this work."

13. *Ibid.*, pp. 72–73.

14. Schindler, *op. cit.*, p. 1820.

15. Francis Vatablus (d. 1547) was the Regius Professor of

Divinity at the University of Paris from 1531 to his death. Milton mentions him in *Tetrachordon*, C.E., IV, 108–09.

16. Biblia Sacra ex Hebraeo et Graeco Latina facta. Altera tralatio vetus est, altera Nova cum adnotationibus. Francisci Vatabli (Hanover, 1605), p. 200.

17. *Synopsis Criticorum*, I, 721.

18. Fletcher, *op. cit.*, p. 27.

19. Qere (קרי) and Khetiv (כתיב) are massoretic terms to describe certain variant readings of the text. The Qere (to be read) were those marginal variants that were to be read instead of the Khetiv (what is written); that is, the marginal reading was to be read instead of the word in the text itself.

20. Fletcher, *op. cit.*, p. 29.

21. John Weemse, *The Christian Synagogue* (London, 1623), p. 29.

22. Buxtorf, *op. cit.*, pp. 2326–27.

23. I Samuel 25:22

24. I Kings 14:10.

25. Aramaic paraphrase of the Hebrew text. The Targum frequently provides a reading which aids in the understanding of a defective passage of the Hebrew.

26. Fletcher, *op. cit.*, pp. 32–33.

27. Schindler, *op. cit.*, p. 1955.

28. Weemse, *op. cit.*, p. 233.

29. Fletcher, *op. cit.*, p. 33.

30. The first of Bomberg's Rabbinical Bibles was published in 1517. The best edition was the Venice edition of 1547–49 which was reprinted in 1568 and in 1617. Buxtorf's Bible is based on the Bomberg.

31. Fletcher, *op. cit.*, pp. 34–35.

32. Johann Hottinger, *Thesaurus Philologicus* (2d ed.; Zurich, 1659), pp. 416–18.

33. Cf. *Of Prelatical Episcopacy*, C.E., III, Part I, 104.

34. *Baal*, or God of the Land, who opposed Yahweh and his mode of worship, was made to read *Bosheth* or "shame." Copyists substituted the word for the word that meant "God of Idolatry." Sometimes it was compounded with proper names. (Hosea 2:16.)

35. Fletcher, *op. cit.*, p. 41.

36. Schindler, *op. cit.*, p. 233.

37. *Ibid.*, p. 179.

38. Grotius, *Annotationes ad Veterum Testamentum* (Amsterdam, 1644), II, 164.

39. Poole, *Synopsis Criticorum*, III, 698.

40. *The Doctrine and Discipline of Divorce*, C.E., III, Part II, 487–88.

41. Both the Septuagint and the Vulgate render זנה less literally than the A. V.:

> *LXX:* καὶ ἐπορεύθη ἀπ' αὐτου η παλλακὴ αὐτοῦ καὶ ἀπῆλθε παρ' αὐτοῦ εἰς οἶκον πατρὸς αὐτῆς εἰς Βηθλεὲμ' Ιούδα

"(And his concubine *departed from him* and went away from him to the house of her father to Bethleem Juda.)"

Vulgate: "*quae reliquit eum*, et reversa est in domum patris sui in Bethlehem."

A.V.: "And his concubine *played the whore against him*, and went away from him unto her father's house to Bethlehem-Judah."

42. Cf. Vatablus, Münster, De Lyra, Marinus, Grotius. Drusius gives:

"*Scortata est apud eum Hier.* Quae reliquit eum . . . . Thargum *sprevit eum:* h.e. inquit R.D. [Kimchi] *despexit eum et abiit ab eo, initque ad domum patris sui* . . . . Non curavit eum, nec abscondit se ab eo dum scortaretur . . . . videndus hic R.S. [Rashi] et Lira quoque."

43. Cf. *supra*, Chapter I, *n.* 37.

Chapter V

1. For a convenient tabulation of such estimates (with bibliography), cf. Taylor, *Milton's Use of DuBartas*, pp. 16, 18.

2. Since the doctrine of creation is theological and not poetical, the literary parallels between *Paradise Lost* and DuBartas's *La Sepmaine*, Tasso's *Il Mondo Creato*, Grotius's *Adamus Exul*, and Gossuin's *L'Image du Monde*, that have been discussed at one time or another in connection with Milton's treatment of matter, have no bearing on the question of the origin of the doctrine for Milton. His ideas on creation were fully developed in the *De Doctrina;* and, whatever the literary coloration of his

expression of them in *Paradise Lost*, they remain the explicit basis for his conception.

3. "As in all of the preceding centuries of Christian history, it was the common doctrine that the world was created from nothing. John Milton stood wholly apart from the general current in regarding the world as an efflux of God." Henry C. Sheldon, *History of Christian Doctrine* (New York, 1886), II, 104.

Actually, what is specifically unique in Milton's position is his textual derivation of the doctrine solely from the first verb of the Bible and his corollary of the annihilation restriction for God. For these, no parallels (or even faint resemblances) exist at all.

4. "Moderni plerique volunt ex nihilo emerisse omnia; unde et ipsorum credo sententia orta est. Primum autem constat, neque Hebraeo verbo בָּרָא, neque Graeco χτίζειν, neque Latino *creare*, idem quod ex nihilo facere significari: immo vero unumquodque horum idem quod ex materia facere passim significat." *De Doctrina*, C.E., XV, pp. 14–16.

5. *De Doctrina*, C.E., XV, 14–16.

6. Ambrogio Calepino, *Dictionarium Octolinguarum* [Latin, Hebrew, Greek, French, German, Belgian, and Spanish] (Basel, 1584), p. 316.

7. Leigh, *Critica Sacra*, p. 30.

8. Andreas Rivetus, *Opera theologica* (Rotterdam, 1651), p. 8.

9. Simon Episcopius, *Opera theologica* (Amsterdam, 1650), I, 345.

10. David Pareus, *Opera theologica exegetica* (Frankfurt, 1647), Vol. I; Hieronymus Zanchius, *Opera omnia theologica* (1619), Vol. III.

11. Including Ibn Ezra. Though Mr. Fletcher (*Milton's Rabbinical Readings*, p. 86) is quite justified in stating that the position of Ibn Ezra (from his commentary on Genesis 1:1) was widely misunderstood. Mr. Fletcher does not maintain that Milton's whole idea of creation comes out of Ibn Ezra but merely that there is a strong suggestion that Milton was familiar with the rabbi's gloss on ברא. Christopher Cartwright exactly paraphrases this gloss in his *Electa Thargumico-Rabbinica, sive Annotationes in Genesin* (London, 1648), p. 3:

"ברא creavit. Aben Ezra ait plerosque interpretes in eâ esse sententia quod hoc verbum significat .... producere rem ex nihilio .... Asserit autem eos haud meminisse istud vers 21 *creavit Deus cete* et illud vers 27 *et creavit Deus* hominem. Quin et tenebras, quae non sunt nisi privatio lucis, a Deo creatas dici, Isa 45.7."

Cartwright, in this same work, cites Rashi and Ibn Ezra as exponents of the bisexual theory of the creation of man:

"Alios autem existimare Adamum et Evam primo fuisse con-corpores, et corpus hoc vocatum Adam, quae vox marem et foeminum simul denotat. Illud igitur, *et sumpsit Deus unam ex costis ejus*, juxta hanc opinionem vertendum ait, *unum ex lateribus ejus*, quia vox צלע etiam latus significat, Exod. 26.20 ac sensum esse, Deus dissecuisse illud corpus, et unum ab altero divisisse. Pro hac opinione citat R. Salom. Rashi & Aben Ezram."

Milton remarked in *Tetrachordon* (C.E., IV, 76):

"*Created he him.* It might be doubted why he saith, *In the Image of God created he him*, not them, as well as *male and female* them; especially since that Image might be common to them both, but *male and female* could not, however the Jewes fable, and please themselvs with the accidentall concurrence of *Plato's* wit, as if man at first had bin created *Hermaphrodite:* but then it must have bin male and female created he him."

Mr. Fletcher (*op. cit.*, pp. 176–79) quite naturally prefers to credit Rashi with providing Milton with this bit of Jewish lore. But even without the Buxtorf Rabbinical Bible, or the DeLyra commentary based on Rashi (*Biblia Latina, Postilla super totam Bibliam* [Venice, 1489], I, 28), or the convenient paraphrase of Cartwright, Milton could have found the exact allusion in the commentaries in Grotius's *Annotationes ad Veterum Testamentum* (Amsterdam, 1644), on Genesis 1:27: "Masculum et Feminam creavit eos. Minum quam conveniant Rabbinorum super hac re explicationes, et ea quae Plato habet in convivio: quae tamen, undecunque profecta sunt, vana esse non dubito."

Considering Milton's fondness for Grotius's commentaries, this last can be considered the most likely source.

12. "Qui dicit ergo creare est ex nihilo producere, neque exemplo probat principium quod aiunt Dialectici. Nam et Scripturae quae afferuntur loca receptam hanc sententiam nullo modo

confirmant, sed contrarium potius innuunt, nempe non ex nihilo facta esse omnia." *De Doctrina*, C.E., XV, 16.

13. "Actio enim et passio relata cum sint, nullumque agens extra se possit agere, nisi sit quod pati queat, materia nimirum, Deus ex nihilo creare hunc mundum videtur non potuisse non obvirium, aut omnipotentiae defectum, sed quia necesse fuit aliquid iam tum fuisse, quod vim eius agendi potentissimam patiendo reciperet. Cumque itaque non ex nihilo sed ex materia esse facta haec omnia, et Scriptura Sacra et ratio ipsa suggerat, necesse est materiam, vel fuisse semper extra Deum, vel aliquando ex Deo. ut extra Deum semper fuerit materia, quamvis Principium tantummodo passivum sit, a Deo pendeat, eique subserviat, quamvis ut numero; Ita et aevi vel sempiterni nulla vis, nulla apud se efficacia sit, tamen ut ab aeterno inquam per se materia extiterit intelligi non potest, nec, si ab aeterno non fuit, unde tandem fuerit intellectu est facilius, Restat igitur hoc solum, praeunte praesertim Scriptura, fuisse omnia ex Deo." *Ibid.*, pp. 18–20.

14. *Ibid.*, pp. 20–24.

15. "Cum igitur Deum omnia non ex nihilo, sed ex se produxisse, Scriptura Duce, videar mihi probasse, progrediendum censeo ad id quod necessario sequitur, cum non solum a Deo, sed ex Deo sint omnia, non posse quicquam rerum creatarum in nihilum interire; Et quoniam annihilationis huis nulla in sacris litteris omnino fit mentio, cur penitus explodenda sit, ad illam supradictam et firmissimam rationem alias quasdam adiiciam. Primum quia prorsus annihilari quicquam Deus nec velle nec proprie videatur posse." *Ibid.*, p. 26.

16. *Ibid.*, XVI, p. 368. Milton is not sure whether destruction of the world, its final conflagration, means the destruction of the very substance of the world or only a change in the nature of its constituent parts.

17. I saw when at his Word the formless mass,
This worlds material mould, came to a heap.

Paradise Lost, Bk. III, ll. 708–09.

.... ride forth, and bid the Deep
Within appointed bounds be Heav'n and Earth
Boundless the Deep, because I am who fill
Infinitude, nor vacuous the space.

Paradise Lost, Bk. VII, ll. 166–69.

18. *Paradise Lost*, Bk. V, ll. 469–74.

19. O. Fock, *Der Socinianismus* (Kiel, 1847), p. 478. "Es liegt wesenlich in der Grundanschauung des socinianischen Systems, dass sie die endliche Welt schon hinsichtlich ihres Ursprungs in ein durchaus äusserliches Verhältniss zu Gott stellt."

20. *Ibid.*, pp. 479–80.

21. Johannes Völkel, a noted Socinian, was the joint author of the Racovian Catechism.

22. E. M. Wilbur, *A History of Unitarianism* (Harvard, 1946), p. 418.

23. Wolkelius, *De Vera Religione* (Rakow, 1630), Vol. II, Chap. IV.

24. "Ius interpretandi scripturas, sibimet inquam interpretandi, habet unusquisque fidelium: habet enim spiritum, veritatis ducem; habet mentem Christi: immo alius nemo interpretari cum fructu potest, nisi ipse quoque sibi conscientiaeque suae idem interpretetur." *De Doctrina*, C.E., XVI, 264.

25. *Ibid.*, p. 264.

26. *Ibid.*, p. 264.

Chapter VI

1. The "Arabian heresy." Cf. Prateolus, *De Vitis, Sectis, et Dogmatibus Omnium Haereticorum* (Cologne, 1581), p. 56; Ephraims Pagitt, *Heresiography* (3d ed.; London, 1646), p. 148; K. R. Hagenbach, *A Textbook of the History of Doctrines* (New York, 1865), I, 217. Psychopannychism, the sleep of the soul, was a milder form of mortalism. Cf. *supra*, Chapter I, *n.* 14.

2. Milton's position derived from his scriptural theology, but many who espoused the doctrine did so more as a matter of polity. That is to say, the refutation of the Roman Catholic doctrine of purgatory could be simply refuted by abolishing any activity of souls in the intermediate state. Such, for example, was the argument of Joachim Stegmann in his anonymously published *Brevis Disquisitio*. The gist of this pamphlet—wrongly attributed to John Hales, of Eton, at the time of the English version of 1653 (entitled *A Brief Inquiry Touching a Better Way . . . . to Refute Papists*), and reprinted as late as the eighteenth century under his name—is that Protestants had in

many instances offered weak defenses against Popery by adhering to the system of Calvin and Beza:

"Wherefore they [the "Papists"] believe in effect that the
Dead live . . . . Now this is the Foundation not only of Purgatory but also of that horrible Idolatry practis'd amongst the
Papists. Take this away, and there will be no place left for the
others. To what purpose is the Fire of Purgatory, if Souls
separated from the Bodies feel nothing? To what purpose are
Prayers to the Virgin *Mary* to *Peter* and *Paul,* and other dead
men, if they can neither hear Prayers, nor intercede for you?
On the contrary, if you admit this, you cannot easily overthrow
the Invocation of Saints." (Reprinted in the *Phenix* (London,
1708), pp. 333–34.)

Stegmann then proves out of Scripture that souls separated
from the body "are neither dead nor live" and consequently
feel neither pleasure nor pain "for those things are proper to
the whole compound."

3. Calvin, *Psychopannychia, qua refellitur quorundam Im-
peritorem error qui Animas post Mortem usque ad Ultimum
Judicium formire putant* (Orleans, 1534); Lutz, Renhardus,
Erythropolitanus (Basel, 1560).

4. Pietro Pomponazzi in his *Tractatus de Immortalitate Animae* (Bologna, 1516), denied the immortality of the soul as a
philosophic proposition. He insisted, nevertheless, upon his
Christian orthodoxy; reason proves the mortality of the soul,
but faith assures him of the contrary. Cf. Fiorentino, *Pietro
Pomponazzi* (Florence, 1868).

5. Most famous of which was *Man's Mortalitie* by Richard
Overton. Saurat (*Milton, Man and Thinker,* pp. 310–22) assumes
that this is Milton's actual source. But Saurat links Overton
with Fludd's pantheism (Cornelius Agrippa is mentioned in the
pamphlet) and so evaluates the mortalism of the *De Doctrina*
with the whole mumbo jumbo of Fludd and the Cabala. "Even
the retraction theory seems to be known to the Mortalists,"
he insists.

6. *De Doctrina,* C.E., XV, 36–38.

7. "Creato in hunc modum homine, tandem dicitur, *sic
factus est homo anima vivens.* Ex quo intelligitur (nisi ab ethnicis
auctoribus quid sit anima doceri malumus) hominem esse animal

per se ac proprie unum et individuum, non duplex aut se-
parabile, aut ex duabus naturis inter se specie diversis atque
distinctis, anima nempe et corpore, ut vulgo statuunt, conflatum
atque compositum, sed totum hominem esse animam, et animam
hominem; corpus nempe sive substantiam individuam, ani-
matam, sensitivam, rationalem; halitumque illum vitae nec
divinae partem essentiae, nec animam quidem fuisse, sed auram
quandam sive virtutem divinam efflatam, potentiae tantum
vitae et rationis habilem corpore organico infusam; cum ipse
homo factus denique, ipse, inquam, totus homo *anima vivens*
disertis verbis dicatur . . . . Quoties autem de corpore tanquam
de trunco loquimur, tum anima vel idem quod spiritus, vel
facultates eius minus principes, vitalem puta vel sensitivam
significat; haud rarius itaque a spiritu quam a corpore dis-
tinguitur; ut Luc. 1.46, 47. I Thess.v.23. integer spiritus, anima
et corpus; Heb.iv.12. usque ad divisionem et animae et spiritus.
Separari autem spiritum hominis a corpore, ita ut alicubi seorsim
integer et intelligens existat, *nec in scriptura sacra usquam
legitur*, et naturae ac rationi plane repugnat; ut infra plenius
ostendetur. Quin et de omni genere animalium dicitur Gen.i.30,
in quibus est anima vivens; et vii.22.omne in cuius naribus
halitus spiritus vitae, ex omnibus quae in sicco, interiit; Nec
tamen idcirco separatam alicubi existere brutorum animam
creditur." *Ibid.*, pp. 38–42.

8. Schindler, *Lexicon Pentaglotton*, p. 1147.

9. Buxtorf, *Lexicon Chaldaicum*, pp. 1376–77.

10. Leigh, *Critica Sacra*, p. 151.

11. *Ibid.*

12. Gataker, *De Novi Instrumenti*, Chap. X.

13. He could have supported his argument today by the same
linguistic evidence.

14. *De Doctrina*, C.E., XV, 216. "For how can the body which
never had any life of itself die?" he asks.

15. *Ibid.*, p. 218.

16. "Gravis itaque hic oritur Quaestio, Theologorum prae-
judicio reiecta potius quam diligenter satis tractata, totusne
homo, an corpus tantummodo vita privetur? Quae quoniam
citra fidei aut pietatis detrimentum agitari potest, sive quis hanc
sive illam tueatur sententiam; quod ex innumeris pene scrip-

turae locis videor mihi didicisse, nisi quis e scholis potius quam ex libris sacris hauriendam veritatem putat, libere exponam." *Ibid.*

17. Recalling the same approach he used in the problem of ברא.

18. "Cum totus homo ex corpore, spiritu et anima constare passim dicatur . . . . primum totum hominem, deinde singulas eius partes vita privari singulatim ostendam." *De Doctrina*, C.E., XV, 218.

19. *Ibid.*, p. 226 *Totum hominem mori probavimus.*

20. *Ibid.*, p. 224.

21. As in 1 Peter 3:19—*By which also he went and preached unto the spirits in prison*—Milton appeals to the Syriac version of "in the grave" for "in prison" to prove that the spirits were dead and accordingly connects the passage with 1 Peter 4:6 *For this cause was the Gospel preached also to them that are dead.*

22. Revelation 6:9, *I saw under the altar the souls of them that were slain.* Milton here argues (as did Gataker) that in the Scripture idiom, "soul" often is used for the whole animate body (*constare ex toto idomate biblico animam pro toto corpore animato plerumque dici*).

23. "Multos variis de causis exercuit hic locus, usque eo ut interpunctionem etiam tollere non dubitarint; ut si sic scriptum esset, *dico tibi hodie*, id est, etiamsi hodie miserrimus et contemptissimus videar esse omnibus, tibi tamen dico, atque confirmo, fore te mecum in paradiso. id est, in loco aliquo amoeno (nam paradisus proprie coelum non est) sive statu cum animae tum corporis spirituali." *De Doctrina*, C.E., XV, 244.

24. Valentine Schmaltz (1572–1622), distinguished Socinian controversialist, shared the authorship of the Racovian Catechism with Völkel and Moskorzowski. Cf. Fock, *Der Socinianismus* (Kiel, 1847), p. 188.

25. From his *De Erroribus Arian*, Chapter XIV. I have used the text quoted in Johan Hoornbeek, *Socinianismi Confutati* (Amsterdam, 1664), III, 489.

26. Josua Stegmann, Professor of Theology at Rinteln, not to be confused with Joachim Stegmann the Socinian, was an anti-Socinian. His book was a collection of anti-Photinian dissertations submitted by students at the University of Rinteln.

27. The term "Photinianism," one of the many synonyms for Socinianism derived from the heresies with which it was associated (hence also, Ebionism, Sabellianism, Samosatenianism), was preferred by German writers. It was derived, of course, from the fourth-century heretic, Photinus, whose doctrines (as may be gathered from the twenty-seven anathematisms of the Council of 351, all but eight of which were directed against him; the works of Photinus are lost) do resemble some of the Socinian.

For those who prefer Saurat's interpretation of "retire" in the sense of "retract" (in accordance with the Zohar) instead of the sense of "at rest" (in opposition to God's movement to create) in the famous lines:

> Though I uncircumscribed my self *retire*
> And put not forth my goodness, which is free
> To act or not,
>   *Paradise Lost*, Bk. VII, 170 ff.

it may be of some interest to know that Photinus held that the Divine Substance can be dilated and contracted.

For an excellent summary and rebuttal of Saurat's interpretation of "retire," cf. G. C. Taylor, *Milton's use of DuBartas*, pp. 38 ff.

For Photinus, Hagenbach, *A Textbook of the History of Doctrines*, I, 253–55; C. R. W. Flose, *Geschicte und Lehre des Marcellus und Photinus* (Hamburg, 1837); and Wilbur, *A History of Unitarianism*, p. 416.

28. *Photinianismus*, p. 544.

29. "Quartus locus est Philipp.i.23. *cupiens dissolvi et cum Christo esse*. ut taceam incertam et variam verbi ἀναλῦσαι versionem, quod nihil minus quam dissolvi significat, respondeo, tametsi Paulus summam statim adipisci perfectionem et gloriam, veluti ultimum suum finem cupiebat, quod et omnes pro se cupiunt, non continuo demonstrari cuiusque animam elapsam corpore, vel coelo vel inferno sine mora recipi: *esse* enim *cum Christo* cupiebat nempe in adventu eius, quem omnes fideles quam primum adfore et cupiebant et expectabant." *De Doctrina*, C.E., XV, 240.

Milton's insistence that ἀναλῦσαι must, in spite of its uncertain and disputed sense, mean dissolution, may very likely have derived from his acquaintance with Gataker's analysis. [Bishop Sumner, even in the presence of Milton's citation of the translation *cupiens dissolvi*, translates Milton's qualification of ἀναλῦσαι, *"quod nihil minus quam dissolvi significat"* as "which signifies anything rather than dissolution" instead of the literal and correct opposite, "which signifies nothing *less* than dissolution." The whole sense of the passage makes this rendition obvious, and it is curious that Milton's paraphrase, *mori et esse cum Christo* (*loc. cit.*), also escaped the notice of the Bishop.]

Gataker (*De Novi instrumenti*, pp. 72–73) comments:

"Atque ita demum ad locum illum supra adductum ex ad Philipp. C I V 23 revertimur ubi τὸ ἀναλῦσαι affirmat. Pfochenium optime exponi possi per *reverti*. et istud paulisper dispiciamus. est enim locus insignis; sed in qo Hebraismus mihi, caecutienti forsan, hac saltem in parte, nullus omnino relucet. Verba sic habet ἔχων εἰς τὸ ἀναλῦσαι καὶ σὺν χριστῷ εἶναι cui et geminum ejusdem adjicere liceat, ex ad Timoth. Ep. 2 C 4 V 6 qibus in locus eis qid το ἀναλῦσαι qid ἡ ἀναλύσις significet, inter eruditos haud perinde convenit. interpretamenta illustriora discutere, haud infrunitum (spero) censebitur.

"Ἀναλυσις itaque qatuor plurimum significata habet. primo resolutionem, dissolutionem, solutionem composita alicujus designat . . . . Qibusdam interitum et privationem natura infert; Vel materia potius privationi obnoxia, retexit et resolvit id qod a causa prestantiori extiterat. atqe hoc ratione *morti* apte satis tribuitur ἀναλύσεως appellatio."

30. (From his *Refutatio Thesium* . . . . *Frantzii* (Rakow, 1614). Hoornbeek, *op. cit.*, p. 492.

31. Smalcius says of Ecclesiastes 12:7 ("the spirit shall return unto God that gave it"): "Spiritus hominis ad Deum redire, testatur sacra Scriptura. at eum vivere vita, ut ait Smiglecius, spiritum, et vel aliquid sentire, intelligere, vel voluptate frui, hoc extra, et contra Scripturam dicitur." Hoornbeek, *op. cit.*, p. 481.

32. *Ibid.*, p. 481.

33. Crellius, *Commentarius in I Corinth.*, *Bibliotheca Fratrum Polonorum*, III, 247 ff.

34. Luther, *Opera* (Wittenberg, 1574), IV, p. 36.

35. *Essentiam Dei nec generare, nec generari.* This axiom from

Lombard was decreed in the Lateran council held under In-
nocent III in 1215, where some of the works of Joachim of Flora
(who thought the doctrine absurd) were formally condemned.

36. Martin Luther, *Opera* (1562), II, 107.

37. William Tyndale, *An Answer to Sir Thomas More's Dialogue, the Supper of the Lord* . . . . (Cambridge, 1850), pp. 188–89.

"*More:* What shall he care how long he live in sin, that be-
lieveth Luther, that he shall after this life feel neither good nor
evil, in body nor soul, until the day of doom?

"*Tyndale:* Christ and his apostles taught no other; but
warned to look for Christ's coming again every hour: which
coming again because you believe will never be, Therefore have
ye feigned that other merchandise."

38. Sleidanus, *Commentarium de Statu Religionis et Reipublicae* (Strasbourg, 1555), p. 242.

Bibliography

Abrahams, Israel. The Book of Delight and Other Papers. Philadelphia, 1912.

Agar, Herbert. Milton and Plato. Princeton, 1928.

Ainsworth, H. Annotations upon the Five Bookes of Moses. London, 1627.

Alger, William Rounseville. A Critical History of the Doctrine of a Future Life. Philadelphia, 1864.

Bailey, Margaret Lewis. Milton and Jakob Boehme. New York, 1914.

Ball, John. A Short Treatise Containing All the Principall Grounds of Christian Religion. London, 1635.

Barker, A. Milton and the Puritan Dilemma. Toronto, 1942.

Bartolocci, Giulio. Bibliotheca magna rabbinica. Rome, 1675–94.

Biblia Sacra Polyglotta . . . . Edidit Brianus Waltonus. London, 1657.

Bibliotheca Fratrum Polonorum. Amsterdam, 1656.

Blau, Joseph L. The Christian Interpretation of the Cabala in the Renaissance. New York, 1944.

Briggs, Charles Augustus. Biblical Study. New York, 1884.

Briggs, Charles Augustus. General Introduction to the Study of Holy Scripture. New York, 1944.

Buddeus, Johann Franz. Isagoge historico-theologica. Leipzig, 1727.

Budé, Guillaume. ΛΕΞΙΚΟΝ ΕΛΛΗΝΟΡΩ. Basel, 1568.

Bush, George. Anastasis: or, The Doctrine of the Resurrection of the Body. New York and London, 1845.

Buxtorf, Johan. Johannis Buxtorf I Thesaurus grammaticus linguae sanctae Hebraeae. Basel, 1629.

———— Lexicon Chaldaic um, Talmudicum, et Rabbinicum. Basel, 1639.

Calepino, Ambrogio. Dictionarium Octolinguarum. Basel, 1584.

Calvin, John. Works. Edinburgh, 1842–53.

Capito, W. F. Institutiuncula in Hebraicam linguam. Basel, 1516.

Cartwright, Christopher. Electa Thargumico-Rabbinica, sive Annotationes in Genesin. London, 1648.

Cartwright, Thomas. Commentarii Succincti & dilucidi in Proverbia Salomonis. Amsterdam, 1638.

Castell, Edmund. Lexicon heptaglotton. London, 1669.

Chillingworth, William. Works. Oxford, 1838.

Clarke, Adam. The Holy Bible. New York, 1833, Vol. I.

Cocceius, Joannes. Opera omnia theologica, exegetica, didactica, polemica, philologica. 3d ed. Amsterdam, 1701.

Corcoran, Sister Mary Irma. Milton's Paradise. Washington, D. C., 1945.

Cory, David Munroe. Faustus Socinus. Boston, 1932.

Cressy, Hugh. Exomologesis. London, 1647.

Critici sacri, sive annotata doctissimorum virorum in vetus ac Novum Testamentum. Amsterdam, 1698–1732.

Davidson, Samuel. Sacred Hermeneutics Developed and Applied. Edinburgh, 1843.

Drusius, Joannes. Animadversionum libri duo in quibus praeter dictionem Ebraicum plurima loca Scripturae interpretumque vetorum explicantur emendantur. Amsterdam, 1634.

—— Annotationes in Coheleth Ecclesiastes. Amsterdam, 1635.

—— Historia Ruth ex Ebraeo Latine conversa. Amsterdam, 1632.

Elias, Levita. The Massoreth-Ha-Massoreth. Tr. and ed. by C. Ginsburg. London, 1867.

Episcopius, Simon. Opera Theologica. Amsterdam, 1650.

Erasmus, Desiderius. Novum Testamentum omne. Basel, 1516.

Essays and Dissertations in Biblical Literature. By a Society of Clergymen. New York, 1829.

Estienne, Henri. Thesaurus Linguae Graecae. Geneva, 1572.

Farrar, Frederic William. History of Interpretation. London, 1886.

Fiorentino, Francesco. Pietro Pomponazzi. Florence, 1868.

Flacius, M. Clavis Scripturae Sacrae. Basel, 1567.

Fletcher, Harris. "Milton and Yosippon," *Studies in Philology*, XXI (1924), 496–501.
—— Milton's Rabbinical Readings. Urbana, Ill., 1930.
—— Milton's Semitic Studies and Some Manifestations of Them in His Poetry. Chicago, 1926.
—— The Use of the Bible in Milton's Prose. Urbana, Ill., 1929.
Flose, C. R. W. Geschicte und Lehre des Marcellus und Photinus. Hamburg, 1837.
Fludd, Robert. Works. Oppenheim-Gouda, 1638.
Fock, Otto. Der Socinianismus. Kiel, 1847.
Frey, Joseph. A Hebrew, Latin, and English Dictionary. London, 1815.
Fullerton, Kemper. Prophecy and Authority. New York, 1919.
Gataker, Thomas. De novi instrumenti. London, 1648.
Gerhard, John. Tractatus de legitima Scripturae Sacrae interpretatione. Jena, 1610.
Gesenius, Wilhelm. Hebraisches und Aramaisches Handwörterbuch Über das Alte Testament. 14th ed. Leipzig, 1905.
—— Hebrew Grammar. Ed. by E. Hautzsch and tr. by A. E. Cowley. 2d ed. Oxford, 1910.
Ginsburg, Christian David. Introduction to the Massoreticocritical Edition of the Hebrew Bible. London, 1897.
Glass, Salomon. Philologiae Sacrae. Frankfurt, 1653.
Gloag, Paton J. A Critical and Exegetical Commentary on the Acts of the Apostles. Edinburgh, 1870, Vol. II.
Grotius, Hugo. Annotationes ad Veterum Testamentum. Amsterdam, 1644.
—— De jure belli ac pacis. The Hague, 1680.
—— Opera omnia theologica. London, 1679.
Haevernick, H. A. C. Handbuch der historisch-kritischen Einleitung in das Alte Testament. Frankfurt, 1854–56.
Hagenbach, K. R. A Textbook of the History of Doctrines. New York, 1865.
Hailperin, Herman. "Intellectual Relations between Jews and Christians in Europe before 1500 A.D. . . ." *University of Pittsburgh Bulletin*, Vol. XXX (1933), No. 2.
Haller, William. The Rise of Puritanism. New York, 1938.

Hammond, Henry. Paraphrases and Annotations on the New Testament. London, 1653.

—— Paraphrases and Annotations upon the Book of Psalms. London, 1659.

Hanford, James. "The Chronology of Milton's Private Studies," *Publications of the Modern Language Association*, Vol. XXXVI (1921), 251–314.

—— "The Date of Milton's *De Doctrina Christiana*," *Studies in Philology*, XVII (1920), 309–19.

Harnack, Adolph. History of Dogma. Boston, 1900.

Hartwell, Kathleen E. Lactantius and Milton. Cambridge, Mass., 1929.

Hoornbeek, J. Socinianismi confutati. Amsterdam, 1664, Vol. III.

Horne, T. H. An Introduction to the Critical Study and Knowledge of the Holy Scriptures. 11th ed. London, 1860.

Hottinger, Johann Heinrich. Thesaurus philologicus. Zurich, 1659.

Hunt, John. Religious Thought in England, from the Reformation to the End of Last Century. London, 1870.

Hyamson, Albert. A History of the Jews in England. London, 1929.

Imbonati, Carlo Giuseppe. Bibliotheca Latino-hebraica. Rome, 1694.

Ives, Charles L. The Bible Doctrine of the Soul; or, Man's Nature and Destiny, as Revealed. Philadelphia, 1878.

Jacobs, Joseph. The Jews of Angevin England. New York, 1893.

Josephus, Flavius. Compendium Historiam Josephi. Basel, 1529.

Kayserling, M. "Les Hebraisants Chretiens du XVIIᵉ Siècle," *Revue des etudes Juives*, Vol. XX (1890).

Kelley, Maurice. "Milton's Debt to Wolleb's Compendium Theologiae Christianae," *Publications of the Modern Language Association*, Vol. L (1935), 156–65.

—— This Great Argument. Princeton, 1941.

Kirsch, Conrad. Concordantiae Veteris Testamenti Graecae, Ebraeis. Frankfurt, 1607.

Knight, G. Wilson. Chariot of Wrath. London, 1942.

Ladd, George T. The Doctrine of Sacred Scripture. New York, 1883, Vol. I.

Landis, Robert W. The Immortality of the Soul. New York
1859.
Lange, Friedrich Albert. History of Materialism. Tr. by E. C.
Thomas. London, 1877.
Larson, M. A. "Milton and Servetus . . . ," *Publications of the
Modern Language Association*, Vol. XLI (1926), 900.
Leigh, Eduard. Critica Sacra. London, 1639.
———— In universum Novum Testamentum annotationes.
Leipzig, 1722.
LeLong, Jacques. Bibliotheca sacra. Antwerp, 1709.
L'Empereur, Constantine. Clavis Talmudica. Leyden, 1634.
———— Talmudis Babylonici Codex Middoth. Leyden, 1630.
Lewis, Clive Staples. A Preface to Paradise Lost. London, 1943.
Lightfoot, John. The Whole Works . . . Ed. by John Pitman.
London, 1822–25.
Liljegren, S. B. "Die englischen Quellen der Philosophie Miltons
und verwandtes Denken," *Beiblatt zur Anglia*. XXXIII
(1922), 196–206.
———— "Review of Milton's Rabbinical Readings," *Beiblatt zur
Anglia*, Vol. XLIII (1932), 377.
Lloyd, J. An Analysis of the First Eleven Chapters of the Book
of Genesis. London, 1869.
Lovejoy, Arthur O. The Great Chain of Being. Cambridge,
Mass., 1936.
Luther, Martin. Opera. Wittenberg, 1554–83.
McColley, Grant. Paradise Lost, an Account of Its Growth and
Major Origins. Chicago, 1940.
Manassah ben Joseph ben Israel. Conciliator sive de conven-
ientia locorum S. Scripturae, quae pugnare inter se videntur.
Amsterdam, 1633.
———— De resurrectione mortuorum. Amsterdam, 1636, Vol. III.
Masson, David. The Life of Milton. Boston, 1859–94.
Mayerhoff, J. Reuchlin und Seine Zeit. Berlin, 1830.
Mead, Joseph. The Works of the Pious and Profoundly-learned
Joseph Mede. 4th ed. London, 1677.
Mercer, J. Commentarius in Genesin. Paris, 1598.
Migne, J. P. Patrologiae cursus completus, series Graeca.
Paris, 1844.
Milton, John. The Works of John Milton. New York, 1931–38.

Moore, G. F. "Christian Writers on Judaism," *Harvard The-ological Review*, XIV (1921), 197–254.
——— Judaism. Cambridge, Mass., 1927.
Morais, Sabato. Italian Hebrew literature. New York, 1926.
Münster, Sebastian. Biblia Hebraica . . . . adjectes insuper E Rabbinorum commentariis annotationibus. Basel, 1534–35.
——— Epitome Hebraicae grammaticae. Basel, 1520.
——— Hebraica Biblia Latina planeque novi S. Munsteri tralatione . . . . adiectis insuper e Rabinorum commentariis annotationibus. Basel, 1534–35.
Mullinger, James Bass. Cambridge Characteristics in the Seven-teenth Century. London and Cambridge, 1867.
——— A history of the University of Cambridge. London, 1888.
Nash, Henry S. The History of the Higher Criticism of the New Testament. New York, 1900.
Neal, D., History of the Puritans. London, 1822.
Newman, Louis. Jewish Influence on Christian Reform Move-ments. New York, 1925.
Nicholaus de Lyra. Biblia Latina: Postilla super totam Bibliam. Venice, 1488, Vol. I.
Nicolson, Marjorie. "Milton and the Conjectura Cabbalistica," *Philological Quarterly*, VI (1927), 1–18.
Orme, William. Bibliotheca Biblica. Edinburgh, 1824.
Overton, Richard. Man's mortality. London, 1655.
Owen, John. The Reason of Faith, or, an Answer to that En-quiry, Whereof We Believe the Scripture to Be the Word of God. Glasgow, 1801.
Pagitt, Ephraims. Heresiography. 3rd ed., London, 1646.
Pagnino, Santi. Institutiones Hebraicae. Lyons, 1520.
Pareus, David. Opera theologica exegetica. Frankfurt, 1647.
——— Operum theologicorum. Tomus I, continens scripta exegetica, sive commentarios in S. Scripturae libros canonicos Veteris et Nov. Testament. Frankfurt, 1628.
Patterson, Frank Allen. An Index to the Columbia Edition of the Works of John Milton. New York, 1940.
Pellicanus, Conradus. Commentaria Bibliorum. Zurich, 1532–35.
Pfeiffer, A. Hermeneutica Sacra. Dresden, 1684.
——— Dubia Vexata. 5th ed. Dresden and Leipzig, 1713.
Philo Judaeus. De opficio mundi. London, 1924.

Planck, G. J. Introduction to Sacred Philology and Interpretation. Tr. from the original German and enlarged with notes by Samuel H. Turner. New York, 1834.

Pococke, Edward. Historia compendiosa dynastiarum. Oxford, 1663.

Pool, David de Sola. "Hebrew learning among the Puritans of New England to 1700," *Publications of the American Jewish Historical Society*, No. 20, 1911.

Poole, Matthew. A Dialogue between a Popish Priest and an English Protestant. London, 1685.

———— Synopsis criticorum. London, 1669–76.

Prateolus, Gabriel. De Vitis, Sectis, et Dogmatibus Omnium Haereticorum. Cologne, 1581.

Rees, T. The Racovian Catechism. London, 1818.

Reland, Hadrian. Analecta rabbinica. 2d ed. Rheims, 1723.

Reuchlin, Johann. Rudimenta linguae Hebraicae. Pforzheim, 1506.

Rivet, Andre. Operum theologicorum quae Latine edidit. Tomus primus. Rotterdam, 1651.

Robbins, Frank Egleston. The Hexaemeral Literature. Chicago, 1912.

Roberts, Francis. Key of the Bible. London, 1675.

Robertson, John Mackinnon. A Short History of Free Thought. London, 1914.

Rosenmuller, E. F. K. Handbuch fur die Literatur der biblischen Kritik und Exegese. Gottingen, 1797–1800.

Samuel, I. Plato and Milton. Ithaca, 1947.

Sand, Christoph. Bibliotheca-anti-trinitariorum. Amsterdam, 1684.

Sandys, John Edwin. A History of Classical scholarship. Cambridge, 1908.

Saurat, Denis. Milton, Man and Thinker. New York, 1925.

Sayle, C. E. "The Purchase of Hebrew Books by the English Parliament in 1647," *Transactions of the Jewish Historical Society*. London, 1915–18.

Schaff, Philip. Creeds of Christendom. New York, 1877.

Schickard, Wilhelm. Horologium Ebraeum. London, 1722.

———— Jus regium Hebraeorum. Strasbourg, 1625.

Schindler, Valentinus. Lexicon pentaglotton. Hanau, 1612.

Selden, John. Opera omnia. London, 1726.

Sewell, Arthur. "Milton's De Doctrina Christiana." *The English association, Essays and studies,* XIX (1934), 40–66.

—— A Study in Milton's Christian Doctrine. London, 1939.

Sheldon, Henry C. History of Christian Doctrine. New York, 1886.

Simon, Richard. Histoire critique du Vieux Testament. Rotterdam, 1685.

Sleidanus, Johannes. Commentarium de statu religionis et reipublicae. Strasbourg, 1555.

Smart, John S. The Sonnets of Milton. Glasgow, 1921.

Smith, Henry Preserved. Essays in Biblical Interpretation. Boston, 1921.

Sokolow, Nahum. History of Zionism 1600–1918. London, 1919.

Spanheim, Frederic. Dubia evangelica. Geneva, 1658.

Steinschneider, M. Die Hebraeischen Uebersetzungen des Mittelalters und die Juden als Dolmetscher. Berlin, 1893.

Stephanus. Robert. Biblia brevis in eadem annotationis, ex doctiss, interpretatibus, & Hebraeorum commentariis. Paris, 1532.

Stevens, David. Reference Guide to Milton from 1800 to the Present Day. Chicago, 1930.

Studley, Marian. "Milton and his Paraphrases of the Psalms." *Philological Quarterly,* IV (1925), 364–72.

Taylor, G. C. Milton's Use of DuBartas. Cambridge, 1934.

Terry, Milton S. Biblical Hermeneutics. New York, 1883.

Thompson, Elbert N. S. Essays on Milton. New Haven, 1914.

Tillyard, E. M. W. Milton. New York, 1930.

Tremellius, Emanuel. Rudimenta linguae Hebraicae. Wittenberg, 1541.

Tulloch, J. English Puritanism and Its Leaders. London, 1874.

—— Rational Theology and Christian Philosophy in England in the Seventeenth Century. Edinburgh, 1874.

Turretin, J. A. De Sacrae Scripturas, interpretandae methodo tractatus. Frankfurt, 1776.

Tyndale, William. An Answer to Sir Thomas More's Dialogue, The Supper of the Lord . . . . Cambridge, 1850.

Ugolinus, Blasius. Thesaurus antiquitatum sacrarum. Rome, 1744–69.

Voss, Gerhard. Historia Pelagiana. Leyden, 1618.

Watson, F. The English Grammar Schools to 1660. Cambridge, 1908.

Weemse, John. The Christian Synagogue. London, 1623.

Westminster Assembly of Divines. The Confession of Faith. Boston, 1723.

Wheeler, G. W. Milton's Literary Milieu. Chapel Hill, 1939.

Whitmore, James H. The Doctrine of Immortality. Buchanan, Mich., 1871.

Wilbur, E. M. A History of Unitarianism. Harvard, 1946.

Williams, Arnold. "Renaissance Commentaries on 'Genesis' and Some Elements of the Theology of Paradise Lost," *Publications of the Modern Language Association*, LVI (1941), 151–64.

Wogue, L. Histoire de la Bible et de l'exegese Biblique. Paris, 1881.

Wolfe, C. Bibliotheca Hebraea. Hamburg, 1715.

Wolfe, Don M. Milton in the Puritan revolution. New York, London, etc., 1941.

Wolkelius, Johannes. De Vera Religione. Racow, 1630.

Zanchi, Girolamo. Opera omnia theologica. Geneva, 1619.

Index

Abrahams, Israel, 46, 108–09
Anabaptists, 75
An Apology against a Pamphlet against Smectymnuus (M), 54–55, 58, 60–62, 111
Antwerp polyglot, 11, 93
Arminians and Arminianism, 38, 104

Ball, John, 27, 100
Bartas, Guillaume de Salluste du, 50, 113
Baynes, Ralph, 49, 109
Beza, Theodore, 10, 43, 98, 118
Bibliotheca Fratrum Polonorum, 89
Bochart, Samuel, 16, 64, 94
Bomberg rabbinical Bible, 62, 112
Briggs, Charles Augustus, 19, 87, 93, 96, 100
Buxtorf, Johannes the elder, 12, 14
Buxtorf, Johannes the younger, 5, 12–13, 14, 60, 77, 119
Buxtorf rabbinical Bible, 12, 49, 53, 54, 56, 57, 61, 62, 63, 66, 115

Cabala, 89, 91, 118
Calepino, Ambrogio, 69, 114
Calovius, Abraham, 19, 96
Calvin, John, 9–10, 19, 43, 75, 118
Cappel, Louis, 13, 14, 15–16, 42, 93
Cartwright, Christopher, 114–15
Castell, Edmund, 20, 96
Chillingworth, William, 2, 10, 24–28, 58
Christian Doctrine, see *De Doctrina Christiana*
Cocceius, Joannes, 18, 95, 104
Complutensian polyglot, 91, 93
Crellius, Nicholas, 83

De Dieu, Louis *see* Dieu, Louis de
De Doctrina Christiana, 4, 24, 27, 39, 43, 46, 51, 52, 88, 89, 97, 101, 102–03, 104, 105–06, 109, 113, 114, 115–16, 117, 118–20; hermeneutics of, 30–37; treatment of the creation, 68–74; treatment of the soul, 75–85
Dieu, Louis de, 20, 96
Doctrine and Discipline of Divorce (M), 64, 90, 96, 113
Drusius, Joannes, 19–20, 58, 65, 96
Du Bartas, Guillaume de Salluste, *see* Bartas, Guillaume de Salluste du

Elias Levita, 12, 93
Episcopius, Simon, 38, 69, 104, 114
Erasmus, Desiderius, 7–8, 9, 19, 91, 98

Fagius, Paul, 69
Faraji collection, 108
Farrar, Frederic William, 87, 91, 93, 95–96
Fletcher, Harris, 5, 33, 46–49, 52–66, 88, 90, 93, 97, 99, 102–03, 106, 107, 108, 109, 110, 111, 112, 114, 115
Fludd, Robert, 67, 89–90, 118
Fock, Otto, 73, 104, 117, 120
Fratres Poloni, *see* Socinians and Socinianism

Gataker, Thomas, 21, 78–79, 98, 119, 122
Gerhard, John, 46
Gersonides, Levi, 53, 64, 65, 67, 92, 110, 111
Glass, Salomon, 64, 93–94, 104
Goodwin, John, 28, 100